The Reticular Society

Ian Alan Paul

Introduction by Serene Richards

The Reticular Society

ISBN: 979-8-88744-180-1 (paperback)
ISBN: 979-8-88744-181-8 (ebook)
Library of Congress Control Number: 2025943646

Cover design by John Yates / stealworks.com
Interior design by briandesign

10 9 8 7 6 5 4 3 2 1

PM Press
PO Box 23912
Oakland, CA 94623
www.pmpress.org

Printed in the USA.

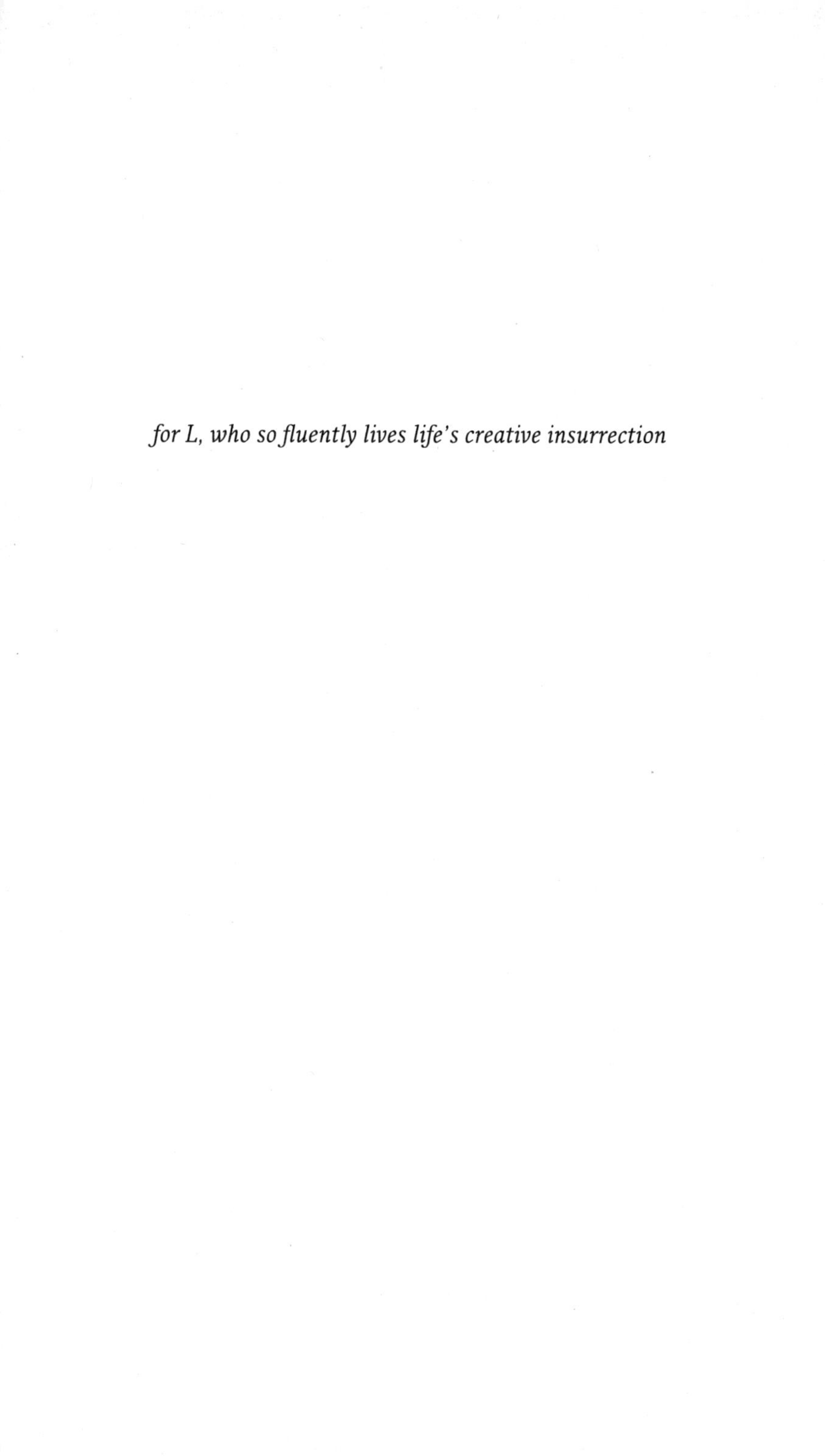

for L, who so fluently lives life's creative insurrection

Contents

Introduction

Serene Richards

The subjugation of the world to its immiseration is every day confirmed though still yet refused. To refuse, after all, is no easy task. It is least of all a solitary endeavour; one can make the personal decision to refuse this or that thing, offer, or right, and while surely satisfactory in certain instances it remains a personal event and so broadly indifferent to the wider world. It is to public events, to the obligatory, ritualised humiliation, that the collective must direct its refusal so that, first of all, there must be the possibility of encounter. Though it is not this collective confrontation with the absolute worst that makes refusal difficult, quite the opposite. A clear glimpse at the horror engenders the confidence and the lucidity to refuse, even making it necessary. Rather, the difficulty lies in the courage to refuse the seductive, the appearance of redemption, that which, as Blanchot writes, "seems reasonable, a solution one could call felicitous."[1] Perhaps refusing the ostensibly felicitous is difficult because, echoing Simone Weil, human beings, irrespective of the countless horrors endured, live in hope

1 Maurice Blanchot, "The Refusal," in *Friendship*, translated by Elizabeth Rottenberg (Stanford University Press, 1997), 111.

that, in the end, good, and not evil, will be done to them.[2] Such is the cruelty of power, instrumentalising our fragility, our seemingly boundless proclivity for fear, and, in an increasingly atomised, hostile world, our longing for security. It does not take much to seduce us, to tickle our wishful conscience that prays for a happy ending, for justice to mean something.

Seductions abound on the merry-go-round, not least in Hollywood. Matt Damon's character, Paul Safranek, in the apparently satirical 2017 film *Downsizing* is seduced by the possibility of transforming his life.[3] A solution to overconsumption and global warming is found by a Norwegian scientist: to downsize, or shrink human beings, so that, being no more than thirteen centimeters tall, they produce less waste, consume less, and are wealthier, since assets go much further given the smaller scale. Paul is motivated by the latter and gets downsized, moving to live in the miniature community, Leisureland. An exemplary solution by techno capital to replicate the same world, capitalism in miniature, where leisure is not promised for all but distributed along class lines. This change without change, a *mouvement sur place*, is a characteristic of *The Reticular Society*. Just as Leisureland comes to be the miniaturisation of the very structures that produce the exploitation of the living, both human and nonhuman, the reticular society is an online inversion of life; as Ian Alan Paul puts it, it is the "networked subordination of life to *what does not live*."

The metaphysical apparatus through which our social, political, and economic strategies are played out is premised

2 See Simone Weil, "Human Personality," in *Simone Weil: An Anthology*, edited by Siân Miles (Penguin, 2005).

3 *Downsizing*, directed by Alexander Payne (Paramount Pictures, 2017).

on arbitrary division and separation of that which it is not possible to divide. What is in question is an abstract, conceptual separation. As Agamben articulates it, this paradigm is apparent in the division between what is real and that which is not, between the possible and the actual, theory and politics, essence and existence, political life and biological life. This ontological machine is not without political and historical relevance. On the contrary, as Agamben writes:

> Without the division of reality (of the 'human' thing) into essence and existence, into possibility (*dynamis*) and actuality (*energeia*), neither scientific knowledge nor the capacity to control and to durably govern human actions, which characterises the historical power of the West, would have been possible.[4]

The scission that renders the machine necessary is not neutral. This is because, in order for the machine to function, what has been separated must in turn be articulated and rearticulated, such that their accordance and discordance represent the machine's rationale. For this reason, if the fabricated space between these ostensible opposites is the space of government par excellence, the ungovernable rejects, refuses, the separation.

Therein lies the originality and urgency of *The Reticular Society*, where the political stakes of the ontological paradigm are unravelled; the reticular is grounded in separation and the subsequent governance of what has been separated. The careful dance of networked togetherness is both infinite and deceiving, for atomisation persists. The

4 Giorgio Agamben, *L'irrealizzabile: Per una politica dell'ontologia* (Piccola Biblioteca Einaudi, 2022), 55.

reticular connects everything "only so it can be separated and subsumed more completely." Such is the perversion of the reticular, that separates only to attempt to bridge back together:

> The reticular society's connected separation, its online ontology, is formalized as the networked integration of its fragmented means of production and control. It advances along the informatic and communicative lines of this formal synthesis: *the circulation of domination* and *the domination of circulation*.

An example is the expropriation of the city: policing and surveillance, exclusion and consumption, in the name of safety, the disintegration of social life in the name of integrated forms of social control. As all of life becomes caught up in the movement of expropriation and domination, the least noticed separation is that of the human being from itself, broken down only to be "further reconstituted in the image of capital, reborn in the industrial form of society's connected separation." In the reticular this movement is heightened, and its seduction ever more appealing precisely because of its hold over and diffusion through information and communication, where life itself becomes subordinate to its dispossession, made possible through the abundance of data and information it itself produces. We are simultaneously producers and consumers of our dispossession, searching for answers and liberation in its captivating reals. In this way the soul is under siege, perhaps catching up with the body and its long history of overt management and control, and the uninterrupted noise saturates: "In the reticular society, lived time is dominated by networked time." This Leisureland with no time or space for leisure is no Playland, that universe of play in which Collodi's Pinocchio would find himself. Like the reticular but in stark contrast to it, Playland, as Agamben writes, also involves an inversion of life, except not by the network but by play. The result is an acceleration of time where, in the midst of a variety of games and the pandemonium of amusement, "the hours, the days, and the weeks passed like lightning."[5] In Playland, the inhabitants are busy celebrating rituals and playing with objects and sacred ornaments while forgetting their origins or purpose, and in this way freeing the sacred and destroying the calendar. It is in play, Agamben writes, that "man frees himself from sacred time and 'forgets' it in human time."[6] In the reticular society, play is reduced to the manipulation of gadgets, and in this way has made ludic play ubiquitous; our relationships, dreams, movements, sleep, reduced to gadgetry. As Baudrillard notes, the ludic might give the appearance of a passion, but it is consumption, no more, no less, and therefore devoid of passion.[7] The gadget cannot attain the symbolic freedom of the toy.

With *The Reticular Society*, there are no illusions or disillusions; it is not a question of compromise or reform. Instead:

> The reticular society understands that so long as revolts *remain connected to what has connected them as separate*, and thus remain captured within and dependent on the very things that dominate them, they will remain as nothing more than a minor error to be eliminated.

---

5 Giorgio Agamben, *Infancy and History: Essays on the Destruction of Experience*, translated by Liz Heron (Verso, 1993), 76.

6 Agamben, *Infancy and History*, 79.

7 Jean Baudrillard, *La société de consommation* (Éditions Denoël, 1986), 114.

What is at stake is a refusal of the reticular and all its iterations. It is not a matter of dismantling but of making the world unrecognizable. An autonomous incipherability to neutralise the totalising abstract calculation of the living toward death. To render the operable inoperable, where the inoperable is "play and rest but also sabotage and strikes." A refusal of the world and its coordinates and presumptions, a refusal of the condition that in order that some might live others must die, to make inoperable all the conditions of immiseration and subjugation, as well as a refusal of the self, produced and put through endless processes of subjectification and desubjectification by the reticular. Far from being passive objects, the innumerable gadgets that surround us often act as intermediaries, as mediators, coming to shape how we understand ourselves and the world around us. There is an intersubjective relationship at play, in a similar fashion to that described by Vilém Flusser on usual objects.[8] It is the user who, most of all, learns and unlearns or adapts. Similarly, for Agamben the apparatus in question always implies a process of subjectification because the apparatus produces their subject and in so doing there is governance, where through a series of practices and discourses, an assumption of identity takes place. So that, as Foucault remarked, "maybe the target nowadays is not to discover what we are, but to refuse what we are. We have to imagine and to build up what we could be."[9] In the words of Marcello Tarì: "Every true strike is also a strike against ourselves: in the same way the working class used

8 See Vilém Flusser, *Petite philosophie du design*, translated by Claude Maillard (Les Éditions Circé, 2002).

9 Michel Foucault, cited in Marcello Tarì, *There Is No Unhappy Revolution*, translated by Richard Braude (Common Notions, 2021), 112.

to strike and struggle for its own destruction, inasmuch as it was a part of capital."[10] There is no return of the same, no complicity or compromise; instead, what is in question is another form of life, another mode of being in the world. As Ian Alan Paul so wonderfully puts it, "Abolition in each instance *dreams of the end of the world* and, in so doing, *dreams of many worlds*."

10 Tarì, *There Is No Unhappy Revolution*, 111.

I

Separation Reticulated

1.

In societies where digital conditions prevail, all of life presents itself as an immense accumulation of networks. What was once lived directly now indefinitely disintegrates into streams of data, fragmented and flowing, reduced to nonliving objects of mere circulation. Inundating culture, politics, and the economy, a calculated deluge of bits and bytes draws every possible experience, activity, and relation ever further online and thus always further elsewhere. The reticular society is nothing less than this *online inversion of life*, this networked subordination of life to *what does not live*.

2.

As capitalism's coordinates drift across webs as data, life finds itself more and more subsumed within the reticular society that aspires not only to network everything together, but to *network everything together as separate*. This communicative invasion advances and infiltrates without end, multiplying its programs and protocols and saturating all times and spaces, propagating its homogeneous logic across sparkling constellations of lives and forms. Falling asleep blanketed within the pixelated glow of notifications softly pouring down a phone, submitting to the indifferent calculations of automated performance reviews at work, tracking the location of a delivery driver in one browser tab while developing attachments to a chatbot in another, and passing through a blinking forest of surveillance cameras and sensors on a subway platform: These are each discrete expressions of an online totality that suffuses everyday life, connecting everything only so it can be separated and subsumed more completely. Within this digital vertigo that circulates all around and cuts ubiquitously through, lives connect *ever more intimately* to what *perennially isolates them further.*

3.

The feeling of the reticular society is of a warm embrace that is also a sharp incision, of a serpentine net of connections that casts informatic shadows over the lives that it amicably ensnares. Lives log on and connect to ever more numerous lives, experiencing a sense of community that remains vividly simulated only so long as they remain online. Its alienation is comforting, its comfort alienating. Identities are cultivated by crafting posts on platforms, the latest catastrophes are commented on online to pass the time, desires swell for content that floats along on feeds, and three or four stars out of five are allotted to one another after transactions are completed as a way of saying goodbye. Partitioned into an archipelago of algorithmic enclaves where only the internet is shared, *lives yearn for and reach out to one another* only to *rediscover and reproduce the networked distances between them*. Each new link advances the separation of life, just as each new separation arises as another opportunity to link between newly separated lives.

4.

The separation of the reticular society doesn't cut between already attached and affiliated lives, nor does the reticular society's integration heave its digital nets over lives that were already atomized and alone. Separation and integration rather work in parallel to produce reticulated lives, informatically dividing and communicatively reuniting society in order to refashion and reformalize life in the image of its connected separation. The reticular society thus does not arrive from a hostile outside but rather arises immanently from within all of the networked relations that draw us to live online together and online apart. Metastasizing across each of life's dimensions as a thick mesh of platforms, programs, and protocols, the reticular society is both *an accumulation of networks* and *an accumulation of a networked relation between lives*, proceeding as a form of circulation that everywhere furthers life's separation. In a singular unbroken gesture, *isolated threads are drawn out to ensnare each particular life* and are woven into a web that *envelops life as a whole.*

5.

In the reticular society, the immiseration of network separation is softened by a liberation of network communication. Digital cuts are stitched back together by multiplying connections, and razor-edged partitions are smoothed over by circulating information. An ambient catastrophe flows between separated existences, tearing open and widening a lacuna that then overflows with software, streams, and screens. As lives search for fleeting escapes from the degradation of lived reality in the ecstatic experiences of online life, solitudes come to be channeled into friend requests, anxieties into virtual therapy sessions, insecurities into online orders, attractions into profile matches, curiosities into algorithmic searches, precarities into gig apps, illnesses into crowdfunding campaigns, euphorias into manic posts, and depressions into infinite scrolls. The resilience of the reticular society arises from this circuitous rerouting of life's desire, through which life becomes ever more drawn toward, dependent on, and devoted to what dominates it, to what life *ought to hate and destroy*.

6.

The reticular society exists as a relation between lives, and more abstractly as a relation between those relations. There is consequently no direct connection between any individual life and the reticular society, but only lives that have been communicatively linked to one another by a totality that has informatically partitioned them apart. Caught within this connected separation, lives are increasingly drawn to live within networked forms of life whose social existence is premised on being ever more online and on their own. Lives lived on networks are persistently dissected into atomized showers of bits and bytes, a uniform downpour of discrete elements that are then recursively reunited within the computed circulation of life's dissolution. In the insulated online comforts of streaming cultural events, personalized platform feeds, and algorithmically curated marketplaces, network communities fleetingly soothe yet inevitably deepen the isolation of their respective nodes, *communicatively anesthetizing a misery that blossoms everywhere digitally*.

7.

Within the coded flows of networked relations, lives steadily come to feel ever more attached to what remains remote and far away, and ever more distant from that which is close and nearby. Life increasingly appears within reach online, and lives increasingly lose touch with whatever fails to circulate there. The protocolic and programmatic truth that now expresses itself everywhere in culture, the economy, and politics is that *only in a society that is so densely and exhaustively networked can lives be so multiply and intensely disconnected from one another and alone.* Like the microplastics that indefinitely spiral and disintegrate in ocean currents, lives are swept up within a streaming disunity that they can float along within but seemingly can never manage to swim out of. Separation everywhere circulates, and circulation everywhere separates. In expanding wakes of subsumption, life is perpetually integrated into the perpetual disintegration of networked life.

8.

In the reticular society, logging on becomes increasingly appealing and seductive as everything becomes more abstracted away from life and more accessible online. Withdrawn into the numerical depths of digital information before resurfacing as the encoded packets of network communication, lived reality comes to be organized by servers, faces appear first as passwords, the means of subsistence are managed by platforms, and physical contact is sought by swiping right. Society is swallowed into the sunless recesses of networked machines and then reappears floating serenely beneath the glossy surfaces of radiant screens. As everything is programmatically drowned and then reanimated as digits flowing across planetary networks, data infiltrates everything and slowly comes to appear as an essential and inalienable attribute of reality itself. Life is steadily impoverished as it steadily enriches networks with data, a poverty that is expressed in an offline world that is always already subordinated and submissive to the connected computers that facilitate its online dispossession. It is only because of a wasteland that spreads informatically and algorithmically, deepening its desert within each life and throughout all of social life, that what is online can appear as an oasis, as a *digitized refuge from the desolation that breathlessly expands*. The reticular society is simply the networked presence of the life it makes absent. It is the form of domination that endlessly communicates what it has captured. It is the circulating simulation of what it has historically stolen away.

9.

Within a formal unity composed wholly of the disunity it sustains, the reticular society evades every attempt to represent it simply because each new line that is drawn to connect two of its points also lengthens the constitutive separation between them. Data visualizations accumulate in government documents, academic journals, climate reports, and financial periodicals, each of which only further aggravates the generalized anxiety surrounding the inability to sufficiently diagram what has come to diagram life so totally. In the informatic depths of network subordination, lives come to feel that they have more in common with *the online abstraction of life* than they do with *lives themselves*. Posts are confused with people and connections are mistaken for communities as relations between lives ever more closely resemble relations between data. Deep attractions are cultivated across live cams, emojis appended to images simulate the presence of otherwise absent lives, workers collaborate to complete algorithmically organized tasks without ever crossing paths, and group chats created to stay in touch with friends slowly become the only thing that is kept in touch with. Daily life is ever more woven into the circuits of ever more numerous data centers, indexing the offline world to an online one that subordinates it. Life steadily and imperceptibly embraces data as itself and as other lives, as its own means and as other lives' means, and thus embraces life *in the alienated form of its connected separation*.

10.

Floating within a totality that aspires to capture everything and lose nothing, lives separately contract and collapse into the infinite densities of informatic black holes, their surrounding emptiness populated only by the stellar debris that carries messages back and forth across the social void. Each new division between lives swiftly branches out into multiplying lines of communication, and each new stream of data steadily carves partitions into what it flows over. Logging on becomes ever more synonymous with living, sustaining the reticulated unity of life's multiplying disunities. The networked convergence of connection and separation, abstraction and subsumption, totalization and alienation, is both the subordinating program and the formal essence of the reticular society. Socially and subjectively, fiber-optically and algorithmically, *integration and isolation work compatibly as components of networked machines*.

11.

As everything solid streams between servers, social relations come to be persistently reformalized as networked relations. This total capture of lived reality is technically accomplished as the online subsumption and separation of everything real, through which all of life's relations are parsed into arrays of individuated links and lives themselves are compressed into sets of isolated nodes. The manifold relations that tie lives to one another and to the world—historically binding together immensely diverse bodies, ecosystems, architectures, economies, infrastructures, and other forms—are partitioned into discrete elements and distinct connections, each of which can be managed, modulated, and modified on its own. This persistent detonation of lived reality into an informatic particulate of circulating bits and bytes ultimately has the effect of making everything feel inescapable and yet unrelated, *seeming to flow everywhere across networks* and yet *fundamentally divorced from every other thing*. Only a totality is capable of creating and sustaining such universal distance.

12.

In the ebbs and flows of society's connected separation, an endless series of global financial crises, climate catastrophes, and political upheavals apparently invade from every direction and penetrate each moment, and yet they are comprehended only as a streaming succession of unrelated events. The wildfire smoke breathed in and out of lungs, the video clips of armed conflicts looping across smartphone screens, the police evicting apartments up and down a street, the cell phone towers camouflaged as trees, the drones hovering above migrant boats at sea, and the mass extinctions predicted for the years ahead all come to be grasped only as the disconnected parts of a circulating whole, as the atomized accumulation of society's online disunification. Subsumed and separated as data flowing between servers, *reality is experienced as a stream of fragments by fragmented lives.*

13.

As the silicon tides of the reticular society rise over and saturate every dimension of social life, data comes to circulate as the relation of all relations and as the capacity of all capacities. Whatever a particular life cannot achieve on its own, *it comes to believe it can do with the data that communicatively orchestrates social life generally*. Digital information modified by algorithms and exchanged across networks directs delivery drivers to apartment blocks, downloads fitness courses to exercise bicycles, sorts visa applications between immigration officers' inboxes, recommends smart televisions and home security systems alongside new lines of credit, logs the subtle movements of service workers across thousands of franchise locations, uploads GPS data from ankle monitors to police databases, counts the number of times a CV has been downloaded by job recruiters, verifies the faces and IDs of people waiting in line at the welfare office, and hosts fraught debates between paranoid neighbors about local package thieves. As all of life's needs and desires—material, emotional, intellectual, existential, sexual, social—are both amplified and accommodated by data on networks, they come to be rerouted into and recognized simply as needs and desires for more data. The alienation developed within the history of capitalism, that historical movement that binds lives together on the foundation of their class separation, finds new form as a networked alienation built on informatic fragmentations and flows.

14.

Traversing cultural imaginations and material realities alike as they saturate all of life's possibilities, networked computers act as the informatic ligaments of society and rewire the microphysics of each activity and relation, cutting the world into and circulating it as data so that a more legible, useful, profitable, trackable, policeable, calculable, programmable, and controllable world can be born. The weightless joy of a night out, the numbing grind of work, the gentle poetry of a friendship, the ritualized sadness of shopping, the wild spirit of a demonstration, the subtle intimacy of an encounter, and the shattering cruelty of war are all metabolized as ever more numerous bits of information flowing between digital machines, tying humanity's fate ever more fully to what fragments it apart online. Within this irreversible movement premised on the accumulation of division and the division of accumulation, data amasses everywhere like dense layers of gloss sparkling atop the skin of everyday life, like dappled drops of sweat shimmering across the surface of social relations, serving as the informatic foundation of *a separate power* and *a power of separation*.

15.

The connected separation of the reticular society steadily compels each life to live an increasingly shared life, but what is shared is only *a divided subservience* to what *subjugates life so totally*. Flowing through the communicative filaments that have been threaded through each of society's dimensions, a tap on a screen here and a voice command spoken into a smart speaker over there interweaves the lived activity of factory workers in Shenzhen, server admins in Palo Alto, rural farmers in Oaxaca, steel producers in Bhilai, nanotech researchers in Berlin, pop bands in Seoul, summer tourists in Barcelona, climate scientists in Antarctica, refinery workers in Bodo, tenured academics in New York, security consultants in São Paulo, market speculators in St. Petersburg, gallery curators in Ramallah, migrant laborers in Riyadh, freelance journalists in Tunis, and data sanitizers in Mumbai. The violent expansion across every continent of capitalism and colonialism, which historically unified the world on the basis of their classed, sexualized, and racialized disunities, now further advances at the informatic scale of bits and bytes that tie everyone and everything together all the more tightly by virtue of their resolution and velocity. Lives find themselves more and more dependent on and yet detached from the other lives that provide for their desires and needs, just as they find themselves more and more subordinated and exposed to the demands and supervision of lives they'll never know or meet offline.

16.

The reticular, that which takes the form of a net or a web or a mesh, emerges historically as the accumulation of online technologies that sever lives apart so that lives can be better subordinated together. Heterogeneous processes of production, consumption, domination, and subjectification all converge on networked computers that synchronize and choreograph their activities, capturing and fragmenting lives informatically so that life can be managed and unified communicatively. Everything becomes maximally available to logistical calculations and online algorithms that persistently reroute flows toward the most efficient zones and around any potential frictions, functioning to lubricate and optimize the larger system while muting the effect of any localized blockage or resistance. A strike in a factory here is answered with the channeling of investments into an industrial zone across the border over there, a flaming barricade in a major traffic artery is corrected for by data centers that dynamically generate new directions for trucks headed to a nearby port, and a cut fiber-optic line is remedied by protocols that suggest new transcontinental paths for packets of information to stream through. Across the profound variation that composes the global economy, politics, and culture, lives struggle to make sense of and transform their shared situation only to repeatedly confront the reality that *society only subsumes them as ever more accessible, expendable, and isolated parts*. Within the twisting coils of this connected separation, whatever social peace is tenuously maintained only signals the agile progress of society's domination, which circulates everywhere.

17.

The precarity produced by society's profuse separation is redirected at every opportunity into a divided means of living online, coupling the proletarian condition with network subsumption. In this meeting of vulnerabilization and communication, lives compete for work, housing, and health care online in a struggle that only *reproduces the unity of their networked division*. A life that is confronted with their own impossibility in an ever more volatile world, that simply cannot survive and endure in its present form, finds themself invited and drawn to become any other kind of life that remains possible online, and thus comes to technically resemble all of the other interoperable components and interchangeable devices that keep networked society connected and running smoothly. Awash in waves of insecurity, lives come to be ever more animated by the need to continuously remake themselves into ever more online lives, searching for connection as a means of partially ameliorating the poverty of their prolific separation. In the reticular society, lives rediscover the foundational truth of their historical situation again and again: *What circulates is what survives*.

18.

While the reticular society isn't synonymous with the internet, the internet is nonetheless the product of a society that already possessed the capacity to imagine it, the means of constructing it, and the desire to use it. The internet thus doesn't inaugurate its own distinct and separate history but rather arises as the networked ensemble of the historical forces it emerged within, as one historical development of capitalist society, which it now continues to develop in turn. Just as a database that tracks arms shipments can be frictionlessly repurposed to track refugee migrations, store inventories, prisoner records, insulin prices, crop yields, viral mutations, porn downloads, or heat waves, a society that was already unified as a partitioned mosaic of factories, slums, colonies, resorts, wages, suburbs, checkpoints, investments, universities, camps, malls, citizenships, mines, banks, megafarms, and jails is also a society that was already prepared in every way to be *further separated and subsumed* on more technically elaborated terms. Capitalist and colonial world history thus were not made obsolete by the reticular society but rather constitutively prepared the ground for it, possibilized it, and continue to live on in updated forms within it.

19.

The reticular society arose in the wake of the historical victory of the digital over the analog. What can be captured and divided numerically can also be stored, computed, and exchanged uniformly and interoperably across networked machines, while whatever eludes quantification and standardized division, what resists counting or cannot be counted or is excluded from counting, simply fails to count at all. Automated background checks, international currency transfers, online concert reservations, autonomous weapons systems, simulated AI girlfriends, biometric surveillance systems, just-in-time logistics, algorithmically generated novels, anti-theft trackers, deceased celebrity holograms, and live-streamed political rallies all thrive informatically in *an enumerated society* that *algorithmically sees in zeroes and ones all that is real*. The digital thus appears as the everything that excludes what it can only register as nothing, as the informatic abstraction of value that codes over all other worth, as the formal foundation for a totality where the network reigns singularly and supremely. Whether exploiting the latencies of global markets with trading software, deploying police units across segregated neighborhoods, streaming clips of dance routines to millions of screens, adjusting the pressure of this or that gas pipeline, or synchronizing janitors' schedules and corporate keynote speeches, the digital is what courses through the informatic arteries of all networked life.

20.

The digital is the formal foundation and organizing principle of all of the reticular society's connected technologies that analyze, reorder, and act on the world quantitatively, through which every dimension of life is enumerated and numbers are weaponized to dominate all of life's dimensions. An assembly line outfitted with clusters of sensors, an amateur drone surveying unruly crowds at a product release party, and a selfie snapped in front of a burning police precinct are captured and divided digitally as data and are then redundantly backed up across servers that make them available for editing, searching, tagging, analyzing, and posting. Within this online circulation of the sensible, a banker sees in a climate model an investment opportunity, a politician sees in a data broker's report a new constituency, and a producer sees in tracked clicks and likes a reason to proceed with another season of an online documentary series. In a society whose manner of being concrete is precisely its abstraction, digitized wages, prices, and bonuses can be continuously modulated by algorithms, and the online movement of advertisements, products, and investments can be coordinated across innumerable nodes. Just as wars are fought to shift lines on maps, society's appearance as data provides the means of perceiving and acting on it as if it were simply digits streaming across servers, adjusting a set of numbers here in order to adjust a section of reality there. When quantitatively abstracting the world as digital information, the reticular society gives birth to the symbolic order it circulates through.

21.

The network acts as the common language of the reticular society's relentless disintegration and subsumption, of a communicative totality opposed to every unity but its own. The commensurability of the digital subsumes life within a technical interoperability premised on uniform divisibility, within which the immense heterogeneity of lived reality can be captured and controlled homogeneously by networked machines. Each bit and byte—whether encoding a citizenship test, a love letter, a store receipt, a prison sentence, a testosterone level, an iris scan, a nuclear accident, a traffic flow, a productivity chart, or a genetic marker—can be exchanged online and algorithmically manipulated exactly like any other. The reticular society without pause integrates these two seemingly opposed yet ultimately complementary gestures, informatic separation and communicative circulation, which continuously split the world open into accumulating banks of data points while simultaneously sweeping them together within its flows that pour through the rifts and crevices of what was just torn asunder.

22.

As data is imbued with the power to assume the place of and circulate as if it were each and every life and thing, a breeze and a car and a laugh and a virus and a crime and a menstrual cycle and a toy and a graveyard and a poem and a border and a river and a first date and a photograph and a skyscraper and a song and a garden can be captured and subsumed together across billions of connected storage devices being written onto and read from at ever higher speeds. Within nets that ensnare and extract, a dance is dissected into a series of coordinates, a smile into a collection of vectors, a one-night stand into a database entry, and a museum visit into engagement analytics. This digital subsumption allows for the abstract and virtual power of networked machines to fold out across the body of the world, reading and writing bits and bytes as if they were constitutive and exhaustive of all being. Throughout the manifold flows of everyday life, *data dominates society as society's representation.*

23.

In the reticular society, the informatic abstraction and manipulation of life are two moments in a recursive process that captures life as data in order to better control it and that controls life in order to better capture data about it. To be data is to be manageable as data, just as being managed means being datafied. The reticular society thus records each gesture, expression, and encounter as digital information in order to shape the execution of new communicative commands and controls, just as algorithms generate and send encoded packets across networks in order to modulate and steer a subsequent series of gestures, expressions, and encounters that offer new data points to capture. The disunity of a society disintegrated into data everywhere advances the unity of a networked one, and the data accumulated about life on networks is also always *an accumulation of a networked power over life*. As fiber-optic undercurrents informatically assimilate society in their illuminated tides and flows, life is submerged and subsumed within a communicative flood of informatically commensurable and algorithmically manipulatable things.

24.

As the reticular society separates and integrates lived reality at the tempo of microprocessors and at the scale of global networks, code written by someone else processually comes to be experienced intuitively and intimately as if it were naturally our own. Toddlers effortlessly learn to swipe across icons on tablets, time spent on platforms leaves the impression of having spent time with people, and constellations of blinking drones are mistaken for the starlight that long ago vanished from city skies. On the bus, in class, during a work break, at dinner, and in bed, lives retreat into screens that appear more alive, ample, and authentic than their surroundings. The more networked computers are integrated into everyday life and the more optimized their interfaces are designed to be, *the more opaque and innate their domination becomes*.

25.

The reticular society produces its own times, spaces, and relations, which are hostile to all others, injecting its machinic form into every life and thing while blighting whatever resists being captured and subsumed. As this digitized colonization percolates across society, what is online ceases to be an addendum to an otherwise offline life and becomes instead simply what is lived, just as taking account of a life is becoming increasingly synonymous with surveying a life's online accounts. Each gesture is coupled with becoming an audience to and spectator of its online circulation, and lives *lose track of whether an action or its abstraction occurs first*. The more a life comes to recognize themself in networked flows and feeds, the less they understand the reality of their own existence. The more the accumulation of data seduces life with its limitless abstraction, the more living desire itself is disarmed. In this totalizing circulation that has no reference beyond itself, whatever algorithmically flashes to life on a screen appears so incredibly vibrant that everything else fades into the cavernous folds of imperceptibility. The sunny poverty of so many European beaches, where the waves shine only as the picturesque backgrounds of online posts, is reflected in a society where people live as online tourists of their own lives, seeing in each and every gesture, affect, and expression only more data, even when they are their own.

26.

As online flows come to feel increasingly familiar, programs increasingly personal, and information increasingly intimate, the reticular society comes to understand everything as a reticulation of itself, and those who live in the reticular society come to understand themselves as reticulations of it. Between uploads and downloads, lags and latencies, scans and streams, the internet continues to be imagined as its own distinct place, but only in order to tenuously sustain the belief in an offline world that is independent and real. Like a search engine that endlessly returns links only to itself, networked computation appears both as alpha and omega, as means and end, as input and output, as cause and effect. In an automated cascade of computed advances, *what is imagined as socially possible becomes indistinguishable from what can be abstracted and manipulated as data online*, prompting the network to introduce itself as the single measure of what a society can be, think, dream, desire, and do.

27.

No one has to believe in the reticular society in order for it to properly function. On the contrary, its smooth performance depends on an inability to distinguish between the reticular society and lived reality. Reality informatically circulates through the reticular society, and in this sense the reticular society is real. Thriving in the contradiction between the undeniably true and provably false, the newly updated and already obsolete, the prolifically sampled and profusely simulated, the expansively infrastructural and molecularly embodied, and the vanishingly obscure and spectacularly aesthetic, it says nothing more than "*that which networks is good, that which is good networks.*" Within the sleepless churn of networked machines, we dream of the reticular society and the reticular society dreams of us.

28.

In the circulation of what has been captured and the capture of what circulates, the reticular society operates axiomatically just as it does algorithmically, abstractly just as it does actually, dominating life by dominating the protocols and programs that life lives within. The fluctuations and flash crashes of global financial markets, the aggregation of carbon dioxide in the atmosphere, the virtual shrapnel rendered for simulated civil wars, the contactless waves of smartphones over payment terminals, the beauty filters layered over faces, the vacation photos uploaded from former colonies, and the anonymous manifestos drafted against this or that totalitarian regime are all subsumed alike within the informatic commensurability and technical interoperability of the reticular society, where the goal is nothing and accumulation and circulation are everything.

29.

In the disorienting spin of the reticular society's recursive whirlpool, everything continuously accelerates and expands only to perpetually arrive nowhere, culminating in lives that are so inundated with information that they are forever out of time, and that are so connected to everything that they remain forever out of place. Each waking moment is ceaselessly flooded by emails, alerts, reminders, crashes, ads, logins, streams, pop-ups, notifications, pings, lags, memes, trackers, invites, GIFs, scrolls, and loads, just as the difference between here and there dissolves in the circulation of data that remains faithful to protocols and indifferent to place. Calendars synchronize with smartphone launches and software updates, and maps dynamically scale to network addresses and user reviews. This networked annihilation of history—within which the ruins and dead of the past are continuously eroded and washed away by the programmed recirculation of the new, stimulating, and urgent—aspires to reroute time until it short-circuits, indefinitely dilating a present that only perpetually accumulates its own desolation. The critical and insurgent task today is thus not to lose ourselves within the machinic tautology that rediscovers itself everywhere and eternally but rather to grasp the reticular society as *the historical movement in which we are caught*, as *the ongoing history of what we must struggle to escape and explode.*

II

A Pixelated Spectacle

30.

The domination and alienation at the heart of the reticular society are the informatic and circulatory expression of what had already been flowing everywhere throughout the capillaries of capitalist world history. Subsuming life that had long ago been cut apart into classes and bound together on that basis, the reticular society reinvents and reprograms the unity of life's disunity online, increasing its resolution, lending it higher degrees of fidelity, and multiplying its circulation. Sexualized and racialized divisions find new form as data, ushering in an age where they can communicatively and algorithmically encroach on facets of social life that had formerly remained beyond the economy's valorization and subjugation. Proceeding continuously with what preceded it, the reticular society appears as both the child of the capitalist mode of production as well as the advancement of that mode of production online. The reticular society is *capital accumulated to such a degree that it becomes a network.*

31.

All of the technologies of capitalism are technologies of separation, and in the reticular society these technologies come to be communicatively linked together and made interoperable. Capitalism's historical divisions are reassigned and multiplied as internet addresses, global trade is managed and monitored by competing algorithms, and enclosure and extraction home in on attention and communication. Whenever or wherever the economy advances, a corresponding network relation advances too. The world that had been spatially organized into centers and peripheries, extractive territories and distribution hubs, urban enclaves and industrial zones, and walled resorts and policed slums now informatically reorganizes itself as a reticulated mesh of links and nodes, just as the concrete and steel of cities have become secondary to the software and databases that orchestrate what takes place within and moves through them. The world that had been temporally organized into work shifts, exam periods, allotted vacations, loathed elections, stressful commutes, prison sentences, and production schedules now further breaks down within processor cycles that submit them to algorithmic optimization and communicative organization, just as employee time clocks have been superseded by screen recorders that surveil and generate reports on the minutiae of employees' mouse movements and clicks.

32.

The spread of capitalism across the whole surface of the earth, which aspired to eliminate all geographic distance, today continues to spread as a network that propagates its own informatic and communicative separations across what capital had violently unified. Lives come to be dominated less and less as particular forms of life—as a woman, a worker, a dissident, a migrant—and more and more as mobile constellations of data composed of online profiles, credit histories, commute patterns, biometric records, ad clicks, digitized visas, viewing habits, and accumulated likes. Hierarchical relations of class domination are reproduced at greater intensities and finer resolutions as they are armed with an incessantly expanding reservoir of informatic objects that circulate voluminously online, sharpening life's online supervision, optimization, and subjugation. The competition among a diverse assembly of technically advanced corporations and governments to more efficiently capture and exploit life is thus only the divided appearance of the networked unity that formally structures and subsumes them. The arrival of the reticular society doesn't mark the twilight of class society but rather inaugurates the *online production, accumulation, and circulation of classes* that are mapped onto ever more multiple and microscopic aspects of capitalist society's historical reproduction.

33.

As capital searches for novel channels to pour through, it scans across territories and lives that have been imbued with ever more numerous sets of data. Each additional bit and byte serves as another input for a fluid power that aspires only to magnify the speed and scope of its circulation, sweeping up anything and anyone that can be integrated into its manifold forms of dispossession, subordination, and accumulation. Even the most obscure, remote, and intimate is subjected to networked subsumption and economic valorization, caught within the digitized capture of online capital, which endlessly abstracts the world as information so as to better submit it to its networked logic. Vast networks of machines are put to use to dynamically provide and deny access, accelerate and constrain flows, start and suspend operations, write and rewrite boundaries, and modify and synchronize sets of axioms and rules, reshaping reality on the basis of information as a means of steering all of life toward increasingly optimized, profitable, and networked ends. Online information abstracts and subsumes the living and nonliving alike, allowing networked systems to track and adjust data center cooling systems just as they surveil and direct commuters driving to drop their kids off at school, objectifying everything as data as a means of making everything resemble and reflect the structure of network relations more completely. As society becomes increasingly premised on *the online management of things*, capturing and manipulating reality as an accumulation of data, all of life is subjected ever further to the informatic economy of the network form.

34.

The informatic forms of abstraction that suffuse life in the reticular society integrate all of the preceding forms of abstraction that were developed in the history of capitalism. Like money, data can readily assume the place of and signify every possible thing. Unlike money, data formally extends beyond the mediation of wages, investments, markets, profits, debts, and prices that Marx theorized so well. Bank accounts, health passes, step counters, citizen scores, reading habits, crypto wallets, streaming choices, affect analyses, digital passports, device IDs, and social media logs harmonize together on servers, conjunctively policing and regulating access to housing, loans, education, health care, transportation, food, and other basic necessities. As digital information circulating across networks allows for political, economic, and cultural realities to bleed together ever more fluidly and indistinguishably, money finds itself accompanied and augmented by increasingly numerous regimes of digital abstraction and is itself ever further abstracted as data.

35.

Data flowing online has facilitated the capture of far more than what the economy had historically been able to subsume prior to the arrival of networked computation, increasingly integrating ever more of life into the online circuits of capital. Investments become tied not only to projected revenues but also to active user numbers, not only to asset portfolios but also to analytic insights. Platforms radically transform housing, transportation, consumption, and production, rendering everything more accessible online and thus exposed to ever more numerous forms of online valuation and exchange. Economic life is broken down into and circulated as microtasks and microtransactions that can be enacted anywhere and anytime so long as there is a network connection. Data is now grasped as one of the dominant weapons of capital, as the abstraction that can algorithmically integrate and manipulate all others, as *the form that can subject everything to its informatic economy*. The forms of value that circulate on networks have the tendency to abstract themselves ever further, extending their digital reach deeper and deeper into reality. A tropical storm, a traffic accident, a spontaneous protest, a home movie, a viral infection, an orchard harvest, a child's drawing, and a bird migration—these are all objects that networks take to be tracked, to be managed, to be optimized, to be made profitable, to be integrated into the *online reproduction of class society*.

36.

In the historical development of the economy's domination of life theorized by Guy Debord, all being was degraded into having, and then all having was degraded into appearing. Social relations became mediated by commodity relations, which were then further mediated on a spectacular basis. In the contemporary and most advanced phase of this development, being, having, and appearing have all been further subordinated to networking, within which every form of social relation is mediated by its digitized circulation. In the historical movement from private property to mass visuality to network activity, society came to be structured by commodities, and then by commercials, and ultimately by codes. In this desolating march from the enclosure and factory to the television and billboard to the smart device and server farm, a lived reality that had already been privatized and spectacularized further separates and drifts away as data. Understood in this way, the reticular society can be seen as *the pixelation of the society of the spectacle* that preceded it, culminating in a newly and more densely mediated society where living, having, and appearing are all subsumed within economies of digital abstraction and circulation.

37.

Pixels exist as the smallest fragments of a digital image, their most discrete and uniquely addressable elements. They can be stored out of sight as data in computer memory or displayed as electric blocks of light on a screen, floating back and forth between numerical abstraction and algorithmic visualization. Pixels can exist as recordings of the world as individual points of data as well as renderings of data as individual points of light in the world, but they also exist as the formal basis for *a fantasy of a world that can be captured, circulated, and computed as if it were simply data*. The reticular society is a society that has come to be organized entirely by this fantasy, a society that is understood as a reservoir from which new data can always be read, as an object on which new data can always be written, and ultimately as a network that facilitates and coordinates the distributed reading and writing of society as data.

38.

The pixel is exemplary of the reticular society's many heterogeneous technologies, which are built on a concurrent individuation and totalization, in which the uniform division of the world into discrete elements facilitates their unification in the flows of online domination. Network abstraction separates and subsumes the world into isolated bits of information, codifying and partitioning life at the highest resolution technically possible in order to circulate as a totality more intricately and intensely over it. *The abstraction of digital information is the formal foundation of the networked relation.* Society's disassembly into pixels thus possibilizes *the online reassembly of a pixelated society*, where each click further partitions lives into individuated and standardized elements and each swipe further advances a networked relation that subordinates life generally. Just as individual particles of light visually bleed together into overwhelming images, pixels are among the digital technologies that give texture and form to the informatic skin that can now be felt across the surface of all social life.

39.

The algorithmic ascendance of pixel over spectacle, of information over image, marks the subordination of the visual world to the programmed activity of networked machines that have little need or desire to appear. Digital photographs circulate through the nested chambers of black boxes. Video files are backed up across servers that are installed without screens. The face and object detections, color optimizations, location IDs, and streaming filters that now all densely suffuse visual culture are only technical artifacts of the transition from a society dominated on the basis of commodities and appearances to a society dominated on the basis of data. The work of art that had lost its aura now also shakes off its appearance, coming into view, but only as a vehicle of what doesn't care to be seen. As the visual function of an image succumbs to the algorithmic function of a computer, as the visual content displayed on a screen is subordinated to the digital tracking of the eye that darts across it, the society of the spectacle finds itself running only as a subroutine of a far more complex apparatus. *What had once been explicitly sensual is now simply an accessory to what only makes sense informatically.*

40.

The reticulation of spectacular relations is now expressed in a society that is increasingly organized by machine vision, automated forms of image capture, transmission, and analysis, which build up a visuality that no human eyes are ever intended to see. Cameras that algorithmically detect, record, and report traffic violations, weapons systems that are programmed to identity and automatically fire on what has been coded as a threat, cameras at airport gates that match faces with boarding passes and no-fly lists, and satellites that scan across territories and track the movement of mined cobalt and local militias all contribute to the construction of an online visuality that is both produced and consumed by networked computers, an informatic form of vision that organizes society based on what algorithms observe, *a reticulated distribution of the sensible* expressed as the separated integration of life's relations and digital perceptions. As an expression of the generalized automation of culture, the economy, and politics, technical relations between machines come to be encoded in social relations between lives, subordinating life ever further to systems composed ever more of the nonliving.

41.

In the reticular society, the spectacular continues to mediate social life to the extent that it facilitates life's persistent datafication, thus furthering the networked mediation of life on that basis. Under conditions of networked capital, the eye ceases to be the foundation of a sensual and creative encounter with the world as it becomes simply another object to be tracked, quantified, financialized, and managed. As Jonathan Crary elucidates in his work, lives still live as spectators of society, separately looking on a separated world, but their spectatorship has been everywhere subsumed within and made secondary to the informatic abstraction of the network form. Shining brightly on screens and dimly secluded in data, the pixel represents *the subordination of visuality to the digitality of online life*.

42.

In the society of the spectacle, lives that had once *seen themselves and one another as lives* come to see and relate to life instead as an alienated accumulation of commodities and images. In the reticular society, this spectacular gaze is endlessly recorded, modulated, and redirected within the digitized calculus of the network form. Online life continues to appear visually, but these appearances are just a fragment of life's social abstraction, of the informatic circulation and computation that rewrite all of life's relations on the basis of nonvisual, digital, and algorithmic forms. Social relations thus remain mediated by commodities just as they do by images, but now these forms appear only as the minor brushstrokes of a far more complex composition that advances its mediation principally on the networked basis of accumulated data. What binds lives together in the reticular society is nothing more than a circulation of information that maintains life's isolation, a growing sum of bits and bytes that communicate and compute the spectacular and commodified alienation of the world, a connected separation that sustains only the pixelated unity of its online poverty.

III

Individual and Informatic Life

43.

If we can sense a symmetry between the totality of the reticular society and the particularity of each of our lives, we can do so only because what holds the reticular society together is what holds each of us together too. Networked computers adjust lights in living rooms and alter moods on platforms, allocate resources between nations and modulate the resolutions of online video chats between friends, generate dialogue for customer service avatars and suggest endings for emailed love letters, set prices for medications and evaluate applications for apartment rentals, back up traffic camera images in the cloud and curate music playlists for afternoon runs. Protocols and programs organize and optimize packets streaming between servers just as they organize and optimize lives streaming through their days, technically annihilating any hope of clearly discerning where life begins and data ends.

44.

As lives come to inhabit increasingly networked forms of life, they live not as free and autonomous individuals nor as the obedient inputs and outputs of machines but rather within the recursive relation that is sustained between the two. Individuals with their own nuanced subjectivities log on, find new outlets for their desires, upload photos of themselves and their friends and their families, express ideas and opinions and jokes and dreams and fears, and in so doing are algorithmically disintegrated into and circulated as larger and larger sums of digital information. This accumulation is then put to use by machines that further subjectify and individuate life on those objectified and informatic terms, steering a desire in this or that direction, imperceptibly reinforcing a particular subjective tendency or slowly suppressing an unwanted behavior based on analyses of the data that has been captured. Networked forms of life live in this perpetual online metabolism, in the recursive cycles of life's *subjectification, identification, and unification as individuals* and life's *objectification, quantification, and disunification as information.*

45.

As each individual comes to be reflected in and refracted through a sea of their dividuality, they find themselves endlessly inundated within *waves of algorithmic desubjectification and resubjectification.* This is ultimately experienced as a deep insecurity, in which different subjective realities successively come to the surface and drown as networks facilitate ever more voluminous and accelerated exchanges between lives and data. Any kind of fixed or rigid identity is a liability in a fluid economy, and so more and more flows are set into motion as a means of ensuring that lives remain compatible, flexible, and variable. The speed at which lives can be deployed to work online also increases the speed at which lives can be disposed of, an algorithmic form of adoption and abandonment that compels lives to persistently adapt themselves in relation to the digital flux of online economies. Profiles, personalities, programs, passions, and protocols all recurrently rewire one another into serpentine knots of lived autonomies and dead algorithms, taking form as an ouroboros that doesn't consume itself but rather recursively coils into the shape of ever more complex and tangled circuits.

46.

The networked integration of life's individual and informatic existences is reflected in counterposed fantasies that suffuse the reticular society. On one side, lives cling to the belief that networks offer the possibility of total freedom, unconstrained expression, and individual actualization, in which living online means being able to freely do, say, or be anything. Just like the drivers who feel excitedly alive only when sitting alone in their cars and who feel wildly free only when traversing the policed lanes of planned highways, the controlled and contoured flows of online life can be experienced as the purest of autonomies. Formally tied to the protocolic openness of network communication, the identitarian openness of liberal democracy, and the economic openness of capitalist markets, the only limits that appear in this reticulated fantasy are the ones online lives might voluntarily set for themselves as they come to feel capable of overthrowing every authority, transgressing every boundary, and seizing every opportunity. The self is comprehended as a venture-backed startup, as an online celebrity, as a fiber-optic pulse of light. As a refuge and escape from the indignities, poverties, and brutalities that populate everyday life, everything and everyone online comes to be understood simply as the means of affirming and amplifying one's true self, as variables of an egotistical calculation that approaches society solely as a means of fully realizing one's own unlimited individual potential. At its most extreme, this fantasy emerges as a life that desires to converge with the network entirely by uploading their consciousness online, escaping death in a digital afterlife that conclusively leaves the offline world behind.

47.

In the shadow of a liberated online life is another fantasy, in which networks seemingly appear as a control mechanism whose surveillance is so omniscient and whose domination is so omnipotent that life becomes lived simply as an effect of networks, as an output and an object and nothing more. In this fantasy there is no such thing as autonomy, only lives that have been wholly programmed by and made inescapably subservient to the networks that now code over every particle of lived reality. The lives animated by this fantasy understand that the backgrounds of their video calls are so seamlessly blurred only because the algorithm has already identified them so totally, and that shopping online feels so gratifying only because platforms have already determined in advance what they want and need. While the first fantasy culminates in an upload that escapes death, this second one revolves around the fear that life is simply downloaded and nothing more, that a networked death has already effectively arrived.

48.

While the fantasies of a digitally liberated and digitally enslaved life arise as subjective responses to the lived experience of the reticular society, they equally fail to grasp its dialectical truth: In the reticular society life is lived both autonomously and algorithmically, both individually and informatically. Online life is structured by this antinomy, by the demand that lives live as servile objects that networks can command and control ever more exactly and that lives live as capacious and creative subjects that networks can subsume and capture ever more supplely. Networks dominate lives as if they were variables of computation, demanding they remain obedient and available for orders and optimizations, and networks sustain and rely on lives that are more than components of machines, demanding they perform the labor, intellect, and imagination that networked exploitation and progress requires and relies on. Everywhere lives consume and produce information and are informatically consumed and produced, and everywhere they use networked machines and are used by them.

49.

Subjects and objects in the reticular society aren't opposed to one another but rather are integrated together in processes of their mutual reformulation and reconstitution. Each successive subjectification and objectification further magnifies the networked domination of subjects and objects, just as the networked domination of subjects and objects further integrates them into the subjective and objective machinery that tessellates its digital pattern across the totality of the reticular society. Exemplary in this regard are ride-hailing apps, which dominate life in both objective and subjective fashions, integrating lives as programmable variables while exploiting lives' autonomies. Ride-hailing apps determine pickup and drop-off locations, generate the step-by-step directions of optimized routes, and instruct drivers to engage in small talk or stay silent, commanding them as if they were simply another interoperable component and informatic object of a networked machine.

Those drivers also feel compelled to work because of their economic precarity and generalized insecurity. They are shown images of themselves being tracked and analyzed as they drive, have to maneuver around obstacles and pedestrians that the car's sensors fail to detect, and struggle to find ways of pleasing their customers, who leave them ratings at the end of their rides, each of which steer drivers to be more disciplined and obedient subjects. Between informatic detonation and individual recomposition, lives splinter into circulating streams of information that they then must struggle to live and survive within.

50.

As individual and informatic life are subsumed and subordinated on networks, degrees of autonomy and domination are allowed to coexist so long as they further redirect lives toward the reticular society's ends. Warehouse workers are closely monitored as they follow illuminated arrows on their smartphones toward designated shelves and bins, just as autonomous container vessels are tracked and guided by satellites from port to port, and both are processed and programmed as compliant variables of global networks. Those same workers also daydream about how they'll spend their wages online, experiment with methods of eluding the systems that track them, stream looping clips of celebrity deepfakes during their breaks, invent more efficient ways of accomplishing their tasks, upload selfies to renew work permits, conspire with their coworkers to steal an occasional product or two, study in remote classes in hopes of being flagged by algorithms for promotions, and joke on social media that they will set the warehouse aflame one day, living in networked forms of life that are both subjectified and objectified as data. It's only when workers stop things from working, when their autonomy overrides their domination and they go on strike or engage in sabotage, that society attempts to definitively expel and erase them from the flows of networked life. Everywhere life finds itself subsumed within networks that aspire to *automate and command lives as objects* and to *shape and coerce them as subjects* in a reticulated cycle, establishing more and more online loops between creative and coded life, between autonomous and algorithmic life.

51.

The networked relationship between the autonomous and the algorithmic is fueled by society's generalized decomposition into discrete data and isolated nodes and generalized subsumption within surveilled platforms and uniform protocols. As institutional forms are distributed as software across growing numbers of connected devices and society networks together the ever more numerous elements of its turbulent global grind, lives come to feel less constrained by fixed structures or strict boundaries and thus experience an amplified sense of their own freedom and autonomy. If a life grows tired of a particular identity, they can invent a new one on social media. If they are overwhelmed by a particular job, they can quit and find another on the gig app on their smartphone. If they feel frustrated, threatened, or exhausted by a particular social group, they can find a sympathetic and like-minded forum online. As relations reticulate out across society in a seemingly horizontal fashion, power in general comes to feel less oppressive and overbearing and more responsive and fluid. Even those lives that are most economically precarious are invited to risk it all on stock-trading platforms, just as lives that are among the most intensely subjugated are invited to channel their own little flows of domination online by ordering a gig worker to serve them by completing some arbitrary task, temporarily alleviating their own despair by further circulating it along.

52.

Within the axiomatic currents of networked society, the control of flows is also what makes them appear to move along freely. As an expression of what McKenzie Wark has theorized as the digitized vectors that increasingly organize social life, the participatory logic of network communication functions to both disperse and consolidate power, spreading itself out across all of those who have connected while concentrating itself in mobile densities of informatic and algorithmic domination, making it endlessly redeployable and reprogrammable. The openness of protocols allows for new forms of tracking to close in, the horizontality of networked communication sustains the verticality of platform architectures, and the dispersed multiplication of users centralizes the authority of a few engineers, moderators, and admins. Power fragments and flows through each networked life, which feels increasingly capacious and free, just as lives find themselves increasingly subjected to a networked power premised on their connection to and subordination within it. It is precisely this simultaneity that must be grasped in order to understand networked power, an unfolding synthesis captured in the concurrent experience of *living on networks* and *living beneath them*.

53.

In networked processes whose conclusions only initiate and promulgate further cycles, subjective experience comes to be felt more intensely as it is informatically objectified more comprehensively. This intensity is expressed in a form of subjectivity that never ultimately congeals around stable norms or predicates, settling into being this or that form of life, but rather is continuously reconstituted—shaped by the communicative potential to become this or that form of life online. Swiping across and unlocking screens, downloading apps and navigating interfaces, a life is invited to become a student and learn a new programming language, to become a patient and track their heart rate on their smartwatch, to become a worker and label some images in a database, to become a cop and stream footage of a crime in progress, to become an activist and click "attend" on an online event, and to become a consumer and buy a recommended group of products, all simultaneously by virtue of the packets that protocolically saturate society. Any sense that a life could actually be anything in a sustained way, that a life might finally settle into the stability of this or that kind of life, is overrun by the sense that a life has the potential to become anyone online. Integrated into relentless waves of algorithmic subjectification and objectification, each life's being decomposes into *multiplying cascades of reticulated becoming*.

54.

The reticular society develops by means of disintegration and reintegration, of deterritorialization and reterritorialization, and of decoding and recoding just as capitalism historically does, but it accelerates and multiplies these processes to such a degree that they become open-ended, flooding and crashing over one another as they recursively intensify and fractalize. Individual identities disintegrate beyond recognition but then are reanimated online as a growing multiplicity of surveilled profiles and accounts. The nation dissolves but then returns as a planetary network of ethnonationalist parties remixing each other's aesthetics and tactics. Masculinities multiply on forums and in feeds and add ever more graduated and nuanced diversity to the gendered hierarchies they sustain. The family explodes into a million new domestic and dysfunctional forms while ensuring that generational wealth continues to flow. Everywhere identities become more intensively mobile and multiple, and more extensively datafied and demarcated. Each successive cycle of society's informatic disassembly and reassembly arrives in the end as *a growing accumulation of data*, facilitating the explosion of new variation that can be integrated into the operation and further development of the network form.

55.

The reticular society approaches every kind of structure as a material to be processually broken down and then reconstituted, scattered apart only to be reconfigured on more advanced networked terms. This informatic fragmentation of society opens the way for a combinatorial reconstitution of what had been captured and circulated, allowing for the digital to imprint itself ever more deeply on what it has subsumed and to add fidelity to its models and codes. In place of fixed positions or stable forms, a networked gesture recursively disorders and reorders society only in order to further substantiate and develop the reality of a networked one.

56.

Within an intensity that never calms, lives are compelled to ask themselves again and again not if they are this or that kind of life but rather *to what degree they are* this or that kind of life, making every possible form of life appear like a volume slider on a screen that can be adjusted indefinitely.

Life is exploited not simply as a fixed resource but as *an open-ended potentiality* that must struggle to *continuously reactualize itself in relation to a circulating power*. Predicates no longer simply add definition to life, but also take form as variables that can be tested and deployed in networked calculations. Every lived moment comes to be animated by the inexhaustible potential to subjectify oneself in new ways online, pushing life to be lived less and less within any set subjective role and more and more within cycles of reticulated becoming that draw lives to reformalize themselves into a diversity of subjective roles as desired.

57.

Subjective production in the reticular society takes on a higher intensity than past processes of subjectification, as a consequence of lives becoming ever more deeply integrated into the very mechanisms of their subjective constitution. Lives don't tend to understand their networked selves as an informatic object that circulates at a distance but rather as an innate expression of their own autonomous activity. Lives everywhere subjectively identify with their data, intuitively understanding that to advance in society they have to advance themselves informatically by chasing algorithmic clout, crafting online identities, and broadening networked audiences. Academics share memes online about their conference presentations, chefs produce tightly edited clips of their latest recipes, politicians snipe at one another's posts, soldiers upload body camera footage of themselves storming trenches for groups of fans, celebrities assemble focus groups to make sure their online apologies will be a hit, athletes upload time-lapses of their training regimens, and musicians game algorithms to generate more streams of their songs as each lived activity comes to be formalized relentlessly in anticipation of its online circulation. As the alienated comes to feel deeply intimate, lives are drawn to work interoperably with what dominates them, learning to efficiently traverse networks just as commodities are dynamically exchanged across the economy, learning to see life as something that is meant *to be circulated online* and thus not as something *to be actually lived.*

58.

What begins as a life putting themself online processually turns into a life concerned with *remaking themself in the image of their networked self.* Life's becoming data coincides with data's becoming life, subordinating society to a networked unity that both masks and manipulates the informatic separations on which it is based. As each and every lived activity finds itself oriented by the activity of networks, as lives are subordinated to the circulation of their online selves, data flows away everywhere only to return again and again *as a weapon subjectively and objectively sharpened against life.* An informatic reflexivity comes to pour through each moment, each encounter, each situation, compelling lives to live ever more fully on the terms of their online forms, to live *ever more complicitly with what dominates them so totally.*

59.

In the final analysis, no clear or stable distinction between subject and object survives this relentless disassembly and reassembly, decoding and recoding, disordering and reordering, of life and lived reality. Life remains never wholly determined nor constituted by the networked relation within which it lives, and yet life can never be neatly distinguished or separated from the networks that are so thoroughly braided through every social relation. Theseus's ship shimmers and glitches as it perpetually crashes ashore, pulverized ever more completely and yet kept buoyant as it is persistently rebuilt using its own digital debris, which accumulates in the currents washing all around.

60.

The primary function of subjectivity in the reticular society is ultimately for lives to work interoperably, to compliantly and responsively work in conjunction and cooperation with all of the other objective and subjective components that populate networks, to work *as if they were simply another connected machine*. An interoperable life is a life that can adopt and readopt different roles as needed, that can be dynamically mobilized and abandoned in order to manage shifting workloads and demands, that can formalize and reformalize themself to fulfill a diversity of functions, that can be optimized in conjunction with the other lives and machines they work seamlessly along with, and that can ever more flexibly work with a diversity of interconnected systems even as they come to be ever more broken by them. Becoming maximally interoperable within the reticular society thus involves becoming maximally useful only to what dominates life, and thus becoming maximally invested within and submissive to it. Interoperability is the telos of subjectivity in the reticular society simply because it submits life to the telos of the networks it is situated within, striving to *erase any meaningful difference between lived activity and the activity of networks*.

61.

Arising within the flows of networked relations and reticulated exchanges, subjective desire itself ultimately emerges as another technology of life's connected separation, drawing lives to integrate themselves ever more fully into their own online subjugation. Browsing through the feeds of social networks and online platforms, clicks and scrolls are captured and recorded as informatic objects so that algorithms can better predict what a particular life desires and is drawn to. Newly equipped with this data, networks then modify and modulate the flows of feeds in order to intensify and modify the way a life's desire is directed and unfolds online. An extra second spent on a particular type of content is recorded and analyzed and becomes the basis for weaponizing that content to further draw life into the feed, delivering it more often as a form of stimulation or provisionally withholding it to cultivate a state of deprivation. A like button pressed here and a share icon clicked there reticulate out and produce links to nearby clusters of networked media, providing lives with infinite opportunities to consume correlated content that algorithmically reroutes them through ever more acclimated channels and attuned flows. In personalized feeds and targeted suggestions, networks take on the appearance of simply delivering to lives what they always already desired, even as *networks imperceptibly become central to the infrastructure of desire itself.*

62.

Lives are most often drawn to what they feel enhances their joy, to what magnifies their capacity to think and feel and imagine and do, to what appears to be alive and to enliven. As a consequence, they come to desire the networks they feel extend and intensify their lives, but that in the end only further subsume them within the further division and dispossession of what they're drawn to, amplifying the networked separation that pulses through the radiant filaments of all networked life. Wellness gurus promise to eliminate anxiety and stress, viral politicians promise to remake the system, cryptocurrency investors promise unimaginable wealth, online fascists promise a sense of belonging, and dating coaches promise an end to solitude, all of which are desired only as a consequence of the profound separation and alienation that mediates social life. Everywhere *lives desire and struggle to overcome their division online*, and yet this movement *only further develops the division they strive to transcend*. Each separation within the reticular society inevitably emerges a second time as a separation within each life, as an internal line of fracture that widens as life's desire circulates further online.

63.

At its most extreme intensities, the reticular society is subjectively expressed in forms of life that have come to be so deeply integrated into their networked domination that they desire only to further compound and encode it, finding themselves drawn not to what magnifies life but to what suffocates it. The lived experience of networked disunity flows into a networked desire to make additional cuts on the cuts of the reticular society, to effectuate violent separations on what has already been separated, to augment and intensify and advance the reticulated domination that already bears down everywhere on life. Incels, ethnonationalists, and TERFs (trans-exclusionary radical feminists) are all expressions of this form of subjective desire, all of which seek to further elaborate the networked separation and domination of life by introducing additional sets of sexualized and racialized codes into its digitized execution, expanding the resolution of the informatic matrices through which society's violence is distributed. In these weaponized subjectivities, lives have had their desire rewired and rerouted by the networks that dominate them to the degree that they strive only to *further separate the domination of the separate*. Just as the officer in Kafka's penal colony found himself so enamored of his torture device that he couldn't resist placing himself inside it, throughout the subjective machinery of networked domination there are wounds that obsessively dream only of becoming knives.

64.

The networked reformalization and reconstitution of desire ultimately arises as the subjective engine of the reticular society, compelling lives to both *further isolate themselves* and *further invest themselves* in networked forms of life. A life's desire for something, desire to become someone, or desire for someone else each comes to be structured by a connected separation to and from what is desired, causing desire itself to be expressed as a formal echo of society's foundational violence. Within subjective unities attracted to society's manifold disunity, lives are lived not against but rather in deep affinity with what captures them. Networks thus function to deprive desire of its liberatory, transformative, and disruptive potential and instead work to transform it into *another technology of pacification, division, and subsumption*. In a life that performs an indifferent cynicism online only in the private desperation of accumulating more shares and masses of followers, in a life that passionately crafts posts about the need to radically transform society and understands this as sufficiently radical on its own, in a life that becomes increasingly attached to lives they would prefer to never meet in person out of fear it would dispel what was felt online, and in a life that navigates and leverages networks to satiate their every need so that the screen itself eventually appears to them as all that's needed, desire remakes life into networked forms of life that long only for the preservation and intensification of their own communicative alienation. Spinoza posited that the fundamental question of political philosophy was "Why do people fight for their servitude as if it were their salvation?" Today we should also ask: "Why do people fight for their separation as if it were themselves?"

IV

Producing Control

65.

While all life is homogeneously subsumed as data on networks in the reticular society, the uniformity of this capture only facilitates the extreme dissimilarity of its effects. It is precisely because of the reality that all life interoperably takes part in the reticular society that particular classes of life can be dominated more intensely within it, encoding extreme hierarchies on what has been captured commensurably. Across ever-expanding databases of differences, the reticular society algorithmically and communicatively oversees the accumulation of immense riches and the distribution of expanding immiseration, coordinates the campaigns of populist politicians and the incarceration of targeted minorities, organizes the manufacturing of VR headsets and the shipment of tear gas canisters, and multiplies the delivery of targeted advertisements and the tracking of pregnancies and abortion medications. Digital separation and networked integration are technologies through which *a reticulated domination can be expressed separately upon what it has networked together as separate*, through which *the violence of a totality can be expressed differently upon what it has totally differentiated.*

66.

The reticular society's connected separation, its online ontology, is formalized as the networked integration of its fragmented means of production and control. It advances along the informatic and communicative lines of this formal synthesis: *the circulation of domination* and *the domination of circulation*. Both fluid and fragmented, accelerated and constrained, creative and coded, multiplicities of economic, political, and cultural flows are at once orchestrated by algorithms and arise as the means of algorithmically orchestrating society. Lives, data, and things circulate ever more openly between the metropolis and the colony, between the factory and the university, and between the detention camp and the shopping center, a circulation whose fluidity is sustained by the controls that multiply within it. This connected separation of the means of production and control render them both more intense and extended, magnifying the *efficiency, accessibility, and tractability* of every element in the system.

67.

The reticular society's connected separation is the historical elaboration of capitalism's underlying social form. Capitalism casts at least two shadows, one political and one economic, which blur together ever more completely as they conjunctively *rein in and repress* as well as *accumulate and dispossess.* Capitalism thus cannot be reduced to an economic system defined exclusively by its modes of exchange, consumption, and production, nor to a political system defined exclusively by its modes of domination, codification, and dispossession. These all rather must be thought together, as overlapping gestures of a single historical movement. Capitalism exists as *an economy that it subjugates*, just as it exists as *a subjugation that it economizes*. Indifferently uprooting and indiscriminately bulldozing diverse forms of life along the way, capitalism's historical advance takes shape in a separated production of integration and an integrated production of separation that render life more productive as it becomes more controlled and more controlled as it becomes more productive. Political economy is just one way of naming the radical inseparability of the means of production and control, of naming *their shared existence as technologies of capitalism*.

68.

Capitalism's historical development has resulted in immense accumulations of wealth, but this wealth, which was collectively produced by separated workers, is itself separated on the basis of the class divisions that facilitated its creation. The enormous increases in productivity set into motion under capitalism could not have taken place without the means of control that both ensured the separation of workers *within the process of production* as well as the separation of workers *from the resulting wealth of that production*. Just the same, the vast control of separated lives in capitalist society could not have emerged historically absent the *separated accumulation of wealth* that provided its material and financial foundation. History is full of examples of how quickly security forces abandon their roles when capitalists fail to compensate them, as well as how quickly places of work radically undo their separated form when managers have been kicked out. The means of control and production are thus everywhere bound to each other on the formal basis of the integrations and separations they conjunctively sustain, realized as the unified separation of society's control and production as well as the control and production of society's separated unification. The result is that the apparent prosperity of capitalist societies is reflected everywhere only in a desolating poverty, that the separated accumulation of wealth is reflected everywhere only in a separated accumulation of the exploitation and domination of life.

69.

The principal function of society's connected separation is to further intensify and expand the means of production and control, distributing capitalism ever more interoperably and increasing the resolution of its operation. As the Critical Art Ensemble saw clearly at the end of the twentieth century, power no longer radiates from any single fortified center that can be sieged but instead aims to multiply and circulate across the whole of the planet in an ever more distributed form, accumulating and dispossessing, separating and integrating, producing and controlling as it flows through ever more numerous channels and lives. There is thus no discrete authority or conspiracy at work, but only an ever more diverse and dispersed multiplicity of competing lives that are all subsumed within the shared formal logic of online capital. A factory is linked to investors, consultants, algorithms, and bosses across the planet, allowing for it to be organized, surveilled, and controlled as if all of its elements were tightly unified, and yet when workers rebel, they find themselves fundamentally separated and removed from what dominates them as financial deals, security contracts, and trade agreements reshuffle across networks and recrystallize into new metastable forms. Wealthy consumers in one corner of the world buy glossy electronics built of metals extracted from mines in another, remaining closely in touch with global supply chains and marketplaces and yet beyond the reach of the toxic pollutants that accumulate in the bloodstreams of laborers far away. Power historically develops less in the form of Hobbes's Leviathan, as an indivisible and singular authority, and more as the continuous production and control of the very water the Leviathan swims through.

70.

The historical development of the means of production and control advanced as the diverse disassembly and reassembly of life, a process that now continues its evolution in networked form. The industrialization of the world uprooted and unsettled vast populations and then concentrated them in cities and factories, radically reorganizing life in relation to new manufacturing technologies and immensely increasing society's productive capacity. This dense concentration of life within the forces of production proved to be dangerous for capital, always threatening to revolt en masse against what now dominated them so totally, and so novel forms of separation emerged to better control the social explosivity that was latent in society's industrial organization. The city itself was remade into a weapon against life, better divided so as to be better policed and surveilled. Streets were redrawn to make barricades less effective and to let armies march through urban centers. Spaces of communal gathering were cut apart into privatized sites that each had their own discretely defined functions and thus could be separately dominated within the industrial city's spatial unification. Each novel integration of life was historically coupled with its own form of disintegration, just as the newly disintegrated fragments of social life were continuously integrated into emerging urban forms of production and control.

71.

The industrial forms of separation and integration that remade urban life extended into factories themselves as it became evident that increases in control resulted in increases in production and that increases in production necessitated increases in control. The introduction of assembly lines and other forms of specialization functioned to separate lives from one another, each of whom now found themself producing ever smaller parts of a whole no single life could hope to comprehend. Among all of the other diverse forms of scientific and technological control that were deployed against life in the factory, long exposure photography was used as a form of informatic capture that broke down and dissected the movements of workers into isolated gestures that could then be rearranged, adjusted, and modulated, ever more supplely blurring the distinction between the motion of bodies and the motion of machines. Forces of production became implicated in worker control, just as forces of control became implicated in the production of new kinds of workers.

72.

The unified disunification of life in the factory took form as the separation of living workers, a constant process of disintegration that allowed them to be ever further integrated into the dead machines of industrial society. The spatial division that had been imposed between lives on the assembly line was further elaborated and reflected in a temporal division as workers were compelled to move their bodies in careful coordination with the tempos and rhythms of machines to avoid being crushed or maimed, slowly discovering that their actions were no longer their own. As part of the historical movement of capital that aspired to render life ever more productive and controlled, lives not only had to be separated from one another but also had to be separated from themselves, learning to see their limbs just as they saw the levers of machines, learning to let the movement of their eyes be carried away by the movement of the factory busily operating all around. Everywhere life was further broken down so it could be further reconstituted in the image of capital, reborn in the industrial form of society's connected separation.

73.

The formal reorganization of the city and the factory into spaces of integrated disintegration, into spaces of production and control, quickly extended far more broadly across all of social reality, finding one of its sharpest edges in the historical invention of the prison. The insurrections that regularly erupted against the capitalist reorganization of life were extremely expensive to repress, not only interrupting the productive process but at times even necessitating the complete destruction of unruly neighborhoods and the mass killing of rebellious workers. As Michel Foucault theorized in his work on disciplinary societies, the prison emerged as a technology that *allowed for the integrated control and repression of workers to be separately enacted*, eliminating dangerous and insurgent subsections of the population without having to pay the catastrophic cost of repressing the city or the population as a whole. Alongside other capitalist technologies such as the colony and the police, the prison thus functioned as a discrete technology of control that was neatly integrated with the technologies of production with which it coexisted. This industrial reformalization and domination of social life culminated in the constitution of ever more separated spaces—factories, prisons, schools, apartments, hospitals—that fulfilled their own separate functions but were all connected together as technologies that reproduced the capitalist whole.

74.

The forms of connected separation that emerged within industrial societies and across the broader history of capitalism are in the reticular society further developed in networked forms. The online refashioning of capitalism has taken shape as the expansion of its means of production and control into ever more numerous dimensions of everyday life, effectuated by networks' circulating integrations and algorithmic executions. What the factory and city had done temporally and spatially, the network form refines informatically and multiplies communicatively. Society is remade as networks further subsume and manipulate it as data, the objective of which is to render each and every person, machine, and object ever more productive as it becomes more controlled and ever more controlled as it becomes more productive. All of life sinks further and further into society's machines, sensed and subsumed as another online input and output of society that can be regulated like any other. The locatability, transparency, and accessibility of everything in a world that has been abstracted as data only exposes everything further to what manages, oversees, and manipulates that data online, subordinating life to the abundance of its informatic dispossession, to the power of what *has been separated from life* but that returns online *in its full unified force.*

75.

The abstract degradation and domination of life effectuated by the network form can be observed in the abject misery of adjunct university professors, those academic workers who are compelled to endlessly valorize themselves within an online economy that only perpetually devalues their existence. Adjuncts must constantly work without pay to lengthen their CVs, to remain immersed in their discipline's online discourses, and to train themselves to use digitized education platforms that provide AI-generated comments for, detect plagiarism in, and algorithmically assign grades to their students' papers. They must also remain willing to circulate between institutions as enrollment numbers climb and fall, to welcome opportunities to teach remotely in virtual classes in the middle of the night for students multiple time zones away, and to restart the online search for new temporary teaching positions every semester as part of the networked immiseration of education. The adjunct in many ways simply has no such thing as free time, because all of their time appears online as an opportunity to further prepare themselves to be further subordinated by their employers. The adjunct also has no space of their own, as even their bedroom appears online as another workplace where they can connect and discuss grades with their students. In a more violent and exploitative circuit of production and control, undocumented farm workers in North America are not only tasked with harvesting greenhouse crops by hand in arduous and toxic conditions, but also are ordered to regularly check in at computer terminals installed at the end of each row they've picked, using RFID wristbands to identify themselves and entering the number of boxes they managed to fill so their labor can be tracked and analyzed by agritech surveillance systems. Those who fail to pick at the proper rates are given fewer days of work, those who remain working must do so ever faster so algorithms don't identify them as inefficient and push them out too, and those who are in any way disobedient can be reported to immigration police, who then affix digital tracking devices to their bodies. From their movement across hypersurveilled border territories, to their work on farms, to their digitized policing, migrants are relentlessly subsumed within interoperable online regimes that function to optimize both their labor and their repression. In these cases and a multiplicity of others, the reformalization and redeployment of the university, factory, distribution warehouse, prison, border, and hospital as algorithms, platforms, and devices makes it ever less clear where they begin and end, extending the means of production and control informatically and communicatively across a totality that subsumes life only as *another minor variable of society's ruinous calculus*.

76.

In networked society, the means of production and control have become more formally diverse than simply the manufacturing of goods or the repression of workers, as now almost every form of social activity is to varying degrees both produced and controlled. Online algorithms increase and decrease various social intensities by modulating diverse informatic flows, aiming to increase consumption in one area of the economy, decrease traffic on a particular road, steer viewers toward a new streaming series, accelerate the adoption of new technologies, discourage people from joining a protest, or modulate rates of employment. All of life is subjected to ever more intense *optimization*, that pursuit of efficiency that is undertaken as the maximization of what works and the minimization of what resists, as a growing set of functions coldly imposed on every form. Pseudo needs and desires are set alight and extinguished algorithmically. Everything appears as part of online flows that can be accelerated or attenuated, amplified or muted. No area of online life manages to escape such calculation and manipulation, to outrun the networked drive toward the endless expansion and intensification of capital's social form.

77.

The networked reformalization of production and control historically emerged in conjunction with the development of logistics as a unified science of managing a separated world. The logistical reorganization of society takes shape not only as the networked harmonization of consumption and production and the informatic management of global supply chains, but also as the online organization of control that aims to increase resilience and decrease risk by algorithmically neutralizing any apparent frictions in a system. First emerging as a military technology concerned with supplying armies on the battlefield and only later coming to be deployed within the economy, the logistical form has now come to be expressed as the application of the supply chain's logic to the domination of society generally, leveraging data collected about the world to further optimize and thus subordinate it. Machine parts are redirected to different clusters of factories just as prison population transfers and the flight paths of drones are fine-tuned. Empty containers are shipped to ports around the world to accommodate fluctuating demand just as a city calls in riot police from another to help suppress a riot. In each case, circulation is deployed as a form of power that dynamically organizes the shape of society's uneven distributions, that contours and calibrates the diverse configurations and compositions of society's connected separation. This supply-chainification of society is one form the networked development of the means of production and control takes, approaching every separated element as a variable to be algorithmically arranged and adjusted in order to sustain the networked fitness of the capitalist whole.

78.

In the reticular society, diverse material flows are coupled with ever more numerous flows of information, densely linking circulations of data with circulations of lives and commodities. Lives, machines, and things are each assigned their own address and ID so they can flow and be tracked more frictionlessly across systems that aspire to make the world *ever more economical*, that aspire to formalize the connected separation of society at ever more precise scales and networked velocities. In the history of capitalism, the unified disunification of the world was at first effectuated relatively cumbersomely and inexactly, expressed as forms of extraction, circulation, repression, production, consumption, and dispossession that suffered from a lack of information and agility. These low-resolution and unresponsive forms of social organization and domination represented a problem for capitalism's forms of accumulation to the degree that they remained inefficient and failed to maximize the separated creation and circulation of value in the system. The network is the form that historically allowed for the connected separation of capitalist social relations to proceed more nimbly and minutely, to be executed at automated velocities and to be expressed at increasingly compact resolutions, cannibalizing ever more of life at the speed of silicon and at the scale of the bit and byte.

79.

The subsumptive fragmentation of the reticular society redistributes power across the entirety of the social field, rechanneling forms of domination into as many streams as there are lives. The technical integration of each particular life into a domination that flows across all life renders power less concentrated and more circuitous, less despotic and more democratic, less fixed and more fluid. The separated and unequal distribution of wealth and power across society's classes—constituting and violently sustaining the hierarchies between the Global North and South, men and women, white and nonwhite, citizens and migrants, among many other binary forms—continues to intensify and sharpen, but it now comes to be further divided so it can be further integrated online. New fractalized hierarchies emerge within each of the dominant hierarchies of capitalist social relations, aiming to establish increasingly nuanced and complex divisions within and between classes of lives. Life comes to be ever more situated within ever more discrete, separated, and complex organizations of domination, while remaining subsumed within the immiserating unity of society's network form.

80.

The networks that informatically and communicatively suffuse society can modulate their diverse means of production and control to varying degrees as they aim to sustain profitable equilibriums and symmetries, but neither production nor control can ever be definitely excluded from capitalism's calculations. A society capable only of control but that didn't produce would quickly devolve into a suicidal power that could only plunder and destroy what already existed, while a society that was able to produce but lacked any control could only be described as anarchy or, if preferred, communism.

81.

The subjective ambiguity that exists for lives on platforms—feeling simultaneously as if they are users, consumers, products, and workers—is simply an expression of the ways in which all of social life is now colonized, of the ways in which each moment is now taken as an opportunity to capture data, control behavior, and create value. While there are remote workers in refugee camps who spend their shifts labeling data for machine learning models and thus directly participate in the production of the technologies that will also be used to subordinate and further exploit them, all of life has now become implicated in the separated constitution of its unified domination as every form of social activity and relation comes to be suffused within and captured as an accumulation of information. The value-form comes to take on yet another shape as data, advancing the digital reconstitution and reproduction of the social totality that reshapes all of life's relations within the circulations of capital. Network production and control are built on this communicative and informatic logic that flows across and reshapes society in its image, synthesizing circulation and domination, steadily steering life toward ever more productive and controlled ends.

82.

As online technologies bring capitalism's means of production and control into ever more intimate proximity and formal alignment by integrating them into ever more interoperable and commensurable forms, they come to be executed at radically diverse scales across society. Digital technologies concatenated and coordinated allow for factories, universities, and offices to be managed online, but also for forms of surveillance and control to home in on individual lives and, even further, on dividuated and disintegrated parts of those lives. Lives come to be approached not only as components of but also as their own means of production and control that can be informatically dissected into smaller and smaller elements to be algorithmically analyzed, surveilled, adjusted, and optimized. Packets are sent to modify a gesture, a mood, and an expression just as they are sent to reorganize an assembly line, an academic committee, and a biotech lab. This technical contraction that sees each thing and life as material to be further broken down and modified is coupled with an expanding circulation that sees the totality of society as another object to be acted on and optimized. Online flows aggregate data and then initiate programs to shift unemployment statistics, voting patterns, consumption trends, and delinquency rates as part of the modulation of society as a whole. The algorithms that perform these analyses and adjustments are strategically directed toward calibrated goals yet remain *formally agnostic*, shifting digits to act on a city's population or a cellular process, a factory or a forest, an appliance or an atom, approaching *all things as if they were commensurable*. Network power scales up and down as needed, homogeneously devouring and digesting the world, submitting reality to the informatic and communicative logic of its universal online exchange.

83.

The network as a technology integrates all of the technologies that historically preceded it, ever further automating and coordinating the operations of many diverse apparatuses.

Borders, surveys, prisons, offices, hospitals, ID cards, warehouses, camps, maps, stores, cameras, and factories are all brought together and gifted informatic and communicative capacities, allowing different executions of domination to work conjunctively as relays, picking up where another left off, or at times simultaneously unfolding as a dense layering of techniques and forms. Just as a clock is not only a mechanical machine that rotates its arms but is also a social machine that mechanically synchronizes economic and political activities across vast territories, with each tick mirrored in a life rushing to work, a prisoner entering a cell, or a train leaving a station, the network is not only a digital machine that orchestrates and organizes packets streaming between servers but is also a social machine that digitally orchestrates and organizes all of society's interoperable lives and technologies, rendering possible the unified domination of the separate that now circulates online.

84.

Debates concerning whether politics are secondary to the economy or whether the economy has been superseded by politics are rendered definitively obsolete by the reticular society, which recuperates them both as its own proprietary and complementary technologies. The means of production and control share as their horizon only the expansion and intensification of the networked relations that facilitate, sustain, and compose them. The reticular society aspires to ensure that its own protocolic foundation remains as the form that dominates all other forms, as the technical reality that organizes everything real, as the unity that subsumes and subordinates the corresponding disunity of the global economy and geopolitics. The online mobilization of all of society's resources ceaselessly functions to intensify and multiply the networked separation and integration of life, to subsume everything further within the means of production and control, to allow *for the accumulation of capital to advance as the accumulation of circulation that is the reticular society*.

V

The Life and Death of Networks

85.

The reticular society's production and control of lives as subjects and objects, as individuals and information, historically culminates in a massive intensification of insecurity that invades every dimension of social life. Caught within the informatics of domination theorized by Donna Haraway, this insecurity is the product of an impoverishment technically effectuated by the networked form that subsumes life only to eventually extract and strip all value from it. As every process of valuation comes to be tied to circulation on networks, and as network protocols remain indifferent to what circulates on them so long as the circulation is properly coded and finds a path forward, *the value of any particular thing on a network races to zero as the value of network circulation itself chases infinity*. Anything that fails to optimally and profitably circulate can be programmatically substituted with any other thing, and so each life is rendered eminently exchangeable, replaceable, and ultimately abandonable by the networks that organize and orchestrate life's collective activity. Like the shoppers crushed in a holiday stampede whose deaths don't close the store's automated self-checkout lines, or the migrant worker suicides that don't interrupt the construction of hypersurveilled World Cup stadiums, *the only thing that remains not superfluous on networks in the end is network circulation itself.*

86.

The connected separation of networks serves as the condition of possibility for the networked devaluation of life, in which life's exposure to network communication also exposes it to network depletion, desolation, and disposal. In *necroreticular flows* that cut across algorithmically distributed gigs and connected places of work, the number of lives integrated together corresponds to the interoperable potential of the reticular society's optimization and domination, *subsuming life* and in so doing *circulating death*. Teachers, programmers, doctors, engineers, artists, farmers, therapists, performers, drivers, and writers can be employed and exploited or disused and abandoned as the distributed variables of economic and political calculations, reprogrammed, repurposed, and eventually rejected along with all of the other corrupted drives, obsolete tablets, dead batteries, slow laptops, and cracked smartphones that pile up as the discardable and disposable detritus of the reticular society. The forms of value that are generated on networks are always everywhere mirrored in the generation of expendable lives that remain connected only as something to be potentially employed and ultimately exhausted, *which remain in circulation only for life itself to be rendered increasingly impoverished by the network form.*

87.

Carefully balanced with the reticular society's necroreticular program is a *bioreticular* one, a form of domination that cultivates and utilizes forms of life that persist *in excess of the variables and components of networks*. In order for the reticular society to dominate life, some semblance of life has to remain that is not yet totally dominated, that is more than a wholly controlled or automated life, that remains as a creative and autonomous force unto itself. The circulation of networks must relentlessly aspire to further subsume life, to ever further capture a living resource that the reticular society can use as an input to train its models on and as activity for it to manage, integrate, and exploit. The reticular society depends on this accumulative recuperation of life, operating as a form of power that insists that lives go on living only as a means of sustaining the very thing that networked society dominates and exploits.

88.

Lives that go beyond their programmed instructions, that deviate away from algorithmically predicted paths, and that develop understandings beyond the analyses of machines are the fuel that the further development of the reticular society requires, the creative force that *the reticular society steals and aims to carry off as its own*. It is because life resists being dominated—that living itself is opposed to the death that domination everywhere aspires to advance—that life can be captured within and recuperated by what dominates it, that its autonomy can remain the elusive object on which new algorithms and programs can be calibrated, tested, and deployed. What lives is precisely what networks aspire to subsume as ever more deadened bits and bytes, as informatic objects whose value is derived exclusively from the circulations of networked exchanges. Life's autonomy and creativity are thus simultaneously what defies domination, what arises as the object of domination, and *what networked domination historically develops itself as a bioreticular and necroreticular force in relation to.*

89.

It would be possible to write a history of capitalism that simply cataloged all of the technologies that arose in response to life's insurgent qualities, a history of all of the diverse apparatuses and architectures that were developed and deployed to better capture and control lives. This history of capitalism's technologies would be more or less synonymous with the history of capitalism's social relations, tracing the diverse techniques and systems that reformalized life on the foundation of capital's development. The reticular society is itself only the most contemporary entry of such a project, emerging as both the social and historical organization of technology as well as the technological organization of society and history.

90.

Within the turbulent contradiction between the bioreticular and necroreticular programs of network society, a life is compelled to work as a compliant component of a machine and thus diminish everything about it that makes it living, and yet it must persistently sustain itself as a life beyond the grasp of the machine and thus cultivate everything that increases the power of life. Lives are expected to take personal responsibility for results and outcomes and yet be totally subservient to commands and controls, are expected to contemplate and reflect but only in response to generated prompts and interfaces, are expected to fix systems that have stopped working properly but not break systems that don't work for them, are expected to compassionately comfort one another while remaining numb to the calculations that collectively threaten them, are expected to maximize their intellect and creativity while submitting them to the targeted outputs and calibrated end states of the systems they are captured within. The reticular society always moves simultaneously in these two directions, advancing as *the affirmation of networks* and *the networked affirmation of life*, as well as *the networked negation of life*, a negation of life *that has become networked*.

91.

In the immiseration of society's connected separation that aspires to annihilate every form of offline life, life's reduction to network waste and reproduction as a network resource are ultimately integrated and technically managed together in online forms of care that provisionally sustain life, but only as a means of further capturing and exploiting it. Meditation apps, fitness sensors, crowdfunding sites, sleep trackers, online therapy, remote consultations, calorie counters, task organizers, and, when it all becomes too much, screen time managers all draw lives *to work on themselves and one another* and in the process *become more networked selves*. Whenever possible, the chains of social interdependence are extended and intensified online, but only as a means of extending and intensifying life's dependence on the networks that surveil, dominate, exploit, and further subsume them. The more lives are dispossessed of and alienated from the means of care, the more dependent life becomes on network technologies to meet even the simplest and most elementary of needs. As society's online means of subsistence and survival also come to preserve the forms of violence that make them increasingly urgent and necessary, novel forms of exploitation, dispossession, extraction, and repression branch out like flash floods across what had been thought to be high land.

92.

The reality that life has not been totally subdued and dominated by networks but rather continues to express its creative autonomy and thus *continues to live* is the enduring contradiction that structures the historical development of the reticular society. Just as lives lived in the deteriorating conditions of work nonetheless share moments of joy and develop ways of resisting and revolting together, or as lives lived in the desolating confines of prisons nonetheless manage to collectively build dreams of and struggles for a world beyond the walls, lives that are lived in the necroreticular and bioreticular flows of networks nonetheless remain connected to all of the creative powers and potentials of life, and thus find ways of living that remain undetermined by what dominates them. In forms of insurrection that burn immanently across every dimension of lived activity, those who are slowly deadened in society's online circulation are also inventing new weapons, solidarities, and poetries. The persistence of life's creative autonomy on networks, that lived potential that the reticular society aspires to capture as its own, is the persistence of something that remains essentially dangerous to network society, of a dimension of life that necessarily is lived in opposition to domination. The reticular society strategically places itself in the separation between life and its potentials, between *life* and its *creative and autonomous force*. It is *within this separation* that life now lives, and it is *against this separation* that life must now fight.

VI

Difference and Data

93.

The reticular society's connected separation is not only its formal and subjective foundation but also its principal means of pacification, drowning conflict in a form of neutralization effectuated by the circulation of information. Networks dominate life and in the process produce different classes of dominated life—women, migrants, workers, queers, criminals, and other racially and sexually coded configurations—but rather than extinguish these differences they are embraced, rather than suppress these differences they are subsumed. The ongoing accumulation of wealth and power in any society necessitates creating the means of defending it, and in the reticular society this defense is formulated primarily not as the fortification of barriers or walls but rather as an invitation to plug in and flow through its gates. Antagonistic differences, all of those differences that threaten to make a difference, are brought online ever further so that they can be fragmented into a pixelated blast of discrete and unique data points, always more multiple and further detached from the lived conditions that produce them. Diffused and defused by a networked inclusion that subsumes in order to subdue, *difference ceases to be dangerous as it circulates uniformly and separately across society as data.*

94.

The difference of the reticular society is everywhere pacified as the difference of what can be captured, circulated, and calculated as digital information, of what can be neatly integrated into the computational and communicative processes of recognition and representation that suffuse social life. The abstract objectification that was expressed across the history of capitalism as an expanding commodification and spectacularization now proceeds as an expanding datafication, in which life increasingly recognizes the social world and increasingly recognizes itself as digital information as everything comes to be ever more densely circulated online. Profiles on online platforms provide the means of making friends, finding dates, and hiring employees, genocidal wars circulate as ever more numerous high-resolution videos and maps, museums offer augmented overlays that display funders' logos and visitors' comments on top of artworks, prison yards become sets for pop dance routines recorded and designed to go viral online, and forests populated by endangered species are digitally scanned and then modeled as serene settings for online games before they are reduced to lumber. The distribution of the sensible is no longer structured by an exclusive policing organized by the order that "there is nothing to see here" but rather by an inclusive capture that demands that everything be seen in ever more immersive and comprehensive detail, *but always first as data.*

95.

The difference of data imposed on life is the means through which the reticular society can embrace, cultivate, and accumulate endless differences while dissolving anything truly different from its own interoperable totality. An exploding diversity of digital objects is sustained by the radical similarity of their form, by a commensurability that allows a city, an economy, a sexuality, a celebrity, an insurgency, an ethnicity, a pregnancy, a symphony, a catastrophe, and a university to be separately enciphered and deciphered as data while remaining formally integrated on networks. Each thing thus becomes described in ever higher and more unique resolutions, digitally opposed to every other thing as a matter of identity and yet fundamentally allied with the symbolic and informatic totality that recognizes and represents all things. Composing the strands of what Tiziana Terranova describes as the large nets that are cast onto the turbulent play of singularities, data allows everything to be uniquely different, but only different within the same informatic form as everything else. The informatic representation and recognition of reality takes on its own increasingly autonomous existence and then submits the world to the circulation of its represented and recognized forms.

96.

Within networked circuits that persistently aspire to read and write all of society as data, informatic forms of recognition and representation come to technically reinforce and resubstantiate one another. The recognition of life as data, through which a life is sensed and recorded according to previously calibrated models and stored patterns, facilitates life's representation and manipulation as data online. Similarly, the representation of life as data is precisely what facilitates the future recognition of life, providing an informatic archive that can be correlated with new data as it's being captured. A tourist entering a theme park is matched with a biometric profile, a voice spoken into a phone is verified and responded to by an AI assistant, and a crowd is read by a satellite as an unpermitted demonstration, all of which are saved and stored to *further consolidate an informatically represented and recognized society*. Each instance of capture advances the digital representation of the world, just as each piece of data renders the world more digitally recognizable.

97.

The enciphering and deciphering of society as data functions to abstractly empty out life, symbolically transforming it into a blank block of memory that can be written onto and read from as needed. Smuggled into English from *sifr*, the Arabic word for "zero," ciphers stand in as the symbolic void on which numerical reality rests, as the empty set within which all other numbers are derived, as the circle *drawn around the nothingness at its center*. They sit as the null half of all binary-encoded data, serve as the condition of possibility of digital computation, and provide the zero that is at the foundation of calculus and thus brings together the infinitesimal and the infinite. As abstract markers of nothingness, ciphers exist only ideally and thus cannot be empirically located or counted in the world. Nonetheless, while there is never an absolute nothing that can be directly referenced, a cipher's symbolic absence can still be linked to the presence of things in the world. When ciphers are deployed in the enciphering and deciphering of life, they simultaneously empty lives out within and tether them to an ideal structure that can subsequently be used to manipulate and dominate their material existence. A life enciphered and deciphered as data is a life that has been abstractly vacated so that data can be freely written onto and read from it, a life that has been caught within the abstraction of an empty form that it cannot live within but that it nonetheless can be dominated by, a life that has been subjected to *the cipher's unreality* that is structurally, mathematically, and computationally weaponized *against everything real.*

98.

As difference is abstracted and integrated into society as an accumulation of digital objects, it ceases to be dangerous as it comes to serve as only another variable that can be algorithmically analyzed and adjusted as needed. As an expression of what Andrew Culp describes as an inclusion that spreads through divergence, open lines of communication embrace each and every life but only on the terms of its discrete datafication, annexing lives only to *partition them apart within the online unity of its hostile expanse*. The more a life's difference is recursively enciphered and deciphered within a form of capture that objectifies differences as digital information, the more a life can interoperably be managed on the basis of differences that circulate across society only as recognized and represented digital objects. Lives thus come to be reduced to and apprehended as dynamic sets of their coded predicates—as tracked arrays of nationalities, medical histories, ethnicities, interests, genders, clicks, classes, behaviors, criminalities, and sexualities—rather than as lives themselves, as lives that have irreducibly complex relations to and live in constant tension with the codes that society historically imposes on them. Everywhere online, relations between lives are determined by *relations between circulating things.*

99.

When captured and circulated as accumulations of informatic objects, living becomes less and less a matter of living in relation to other lives who may share particular dimensions of their lived condition, who may *have common reasons to revolt against what dominates them in common*, and more and more a matter of living a life whose difference is something only to be recognized and represented, only *to be compared, exchanged, labeled, modeled, computed, and evaluated*, only to be enciphered and deciphered as data. Social media accounts, digitized government IDs, dating profiles, police databases, and online surveys all invite and accumulate an ever-growing number of identities, measurements, categories, predicates, and descriptions, becoming ever more attentive and accommodating of difference but only as a means of better individuating and isolating life on those terms. All forms of conflict between society and different classes of life are thus *dissipated and shifted away from their oppositional character* and toward their absorption in a *circulating commensurability that aims to impose tranquility where there would otherwise be turmoil*, to remake life into ever more productive and controlled forms, to separate hostile differences informatically so they can be integrated on more interoperable and manageable terms.

100.

As difference is separated, multiplied, exchanged, and thus effectively neutralized as digital information, as it comes to be *expressed in the form of society's connected separation*, everything comes to feel both more estranged and more familiar as everything is informatically represented and circulated in ever higher resolution and detail. Flattened out into the abstract equality of data, the differences between lives effectively dissolve as they flow uniformly through feeds, equally subsumed and equally subdued. Posts and images shared by lovers, coworkers, neighbors, parents, advertisers, strangers, and celebrities all take up the same number of pixels on a screen as they are scrolled past, just as a notification from a boss on a smartphone appears equally alongside notifications from a childhood friend, a shopping app, a doctor, an operating system update, a police department, a storm alert, and a local politician. The reticular society's informatic form of difference facilitates the flow of endless novelty that nonetheless loses all distinctness, accommodating the uniform diversity of everything so that nothing but the same ever appears, integrating every form of possible difference as data as a means of relegating anything truly different to the realm of its own social impossibility.

101.

In the reticular society, lived time is dominated by networked time. Each day is orchestrated by a unified circulation of uniform moments so that everything remains synchronized online, so that the whole of the world lives within the same algorithmic time and that each day is made commensurable with every other. The poetry of time, that lived time that cannot be held on to but only ever inhabited, comes under relentless assault from programs and protocols. The first glimpse of morning light, an idle wait for a bus, the scheduled exam at school, an exhausting shift at work, the last drink at a bar, and a lingering thought in bed are all consumed together within the calculated cadence of online life and made available for analysis and optimization. Networked time ushers in a history in which only society's connected separation can progress, in which the irreversible time of capitalist accumulation and class division codes over any and all lived time. Each moment is subsumed as another abstract and exchangeable part of the algorithmic and circulating whole and then deployed to reproduce the social reality and temporality of the network form. *Everything that exists circulates* only to ensure that *nothing but what already circulates can ever possibly exist.*

102.

Throughout the coded channels of the reticular society, protocols ensure that what flows across networks as disassembled and dispersed packets of information are always reassembled at their destinations in the same precise order they began. The whole of the internet relies on this encoded operation that enforces and reproduces a precise resemblance between what was sent and received, facilitating a circulation of the different that is formally premised entirely on similitude. The apparent diversity of communication on networks is thus always secondary to this programmed similarity that sustains them, in which an abundance of content flows smoothly over a formal homogeneity that sits like a binary wasteland below. As even the most distant reaches of the world are swiftly delivered and brought close as packets of data, as the means of technological reproduction come to be expressed protocolically as the means of technological communication, the differences of the world are subsumed ever further and thus wither away. The perpetual flow of new content online is thus only the veneer of the uniform technologies that govern it, of the reticular society that subsumes all diversity in the coded flows of its informatic commensurability and technical interoperability. Unlike Heraclitus's river, which is an endless stream of difference, on networks everything circulates only to remain the same.

103.

The translation of life's difference into data ultimately is undertaken only in order to preclude the possibility that difference might arise as the basis on which life might *collectively confront society*, is undertaken only to partition *a difference that is lived* into a collection of informatic objects that can be *weaponized against life as data*. The movement that transforms life's difference into encipherable and decipherable digits is thus the same movement that transforms the adversarial into the amicable and the conflictual into the commensurable, within which difference appears to incessantly multiply and increase in an online diversity of informatic objects that results only in difference's total pacification and neutralization. Lives that would otherwise *wildly and collectively lash out* against the reticular society, all of those immensely singular lives who nonetheless *have a shared interest in dismantling and destroying what dominates them in common*, are thus integrated only so those lives can be recognized and represented as, deciphered and enciphered as—and thus subsumed and dominated as—data.

104.

In contrast to the informatically recognized and represented differences of the reticular society, the difference of life nonetheless persists as a form of difference that is opposed and irreducible to identity and representation, as a form of difference that cannot ever be cleanly enciphered nor deciphered but can only ever be encountered in ways that lack discrete resolution or final definition, as a form of difference that *cannot be informatically captured but only potentially lived*. This difference is expressed as what Gilles Deleuze called *an impersonal and yet singular life*, a life freed from all individual, subjective, and objective existence. The difference of life can perhaps be encountered most palpably in experiences of intense intimacy and love, in which a life becomes drawn to and takes joy not in the way another life has been coded as different, differences that can easily be located and recognized in any number of similarly different lives, but rather in a life's potential, which is in itself singularly different and remains beyond all capture.

105.

The forms of intimacy that arise from the difference of life aren't experienced as attractions to a defined and discrete life—a life that has been coded and predicated in this or that way, a life whose formal contours are already clearly set—but rather are experienced as forces that pull on life's being, that intensely draw life to become something unknown in relation to another life or lives that remain equally unknowable. It is precisely when lives approach and come ever closer to one another, after all, that their boundaries lose focus, that they become ever less surveyable, ever less identifiable, ever less recognizable. This is precisely why death is felt so acutely, not because of a loss of information or codes that in fact do survive the end of a life—haunting the living as zombie social media profiles, as data stored in machine learning models, and as bank and government records—but rather by a loss of what *exists only as potential in a life*, of what *gives form rather than is formed* and thus *cannot be frozen or fixed in symbols or codes*. An artist's works may remain cataloged, priced, digitized, and insured in offshore vaults long after they're dead, but the autonomous and creative force that was particular to that life, the virtual potential that is perhaps more real than any of its actual expressions, always remains dazzlingly fugitive to all forms of discrete capture that would take it as an object to be privately and securely stowed away.

106.

Beyond the intimacy that arises between one life and another, the difference of life can equally be found in moments when resistance and revolt spill into the streets, in which a love is found and shared in a collective and common experience that threatens domination precisely because of the way it lacks definition, because of the way it cannot be so easily recognized or represented as a discrete difference or set of differences but as something irresolvably and indivisibly *different in itself*. Erupting as the potential of what has not been informatically accounted for or integrated into the circulatory management of society, revolts reveal the contingency of the totality they emerge within, unsettling the coded relations between what lives and what dominates. As revolts disorder the situations they unfold within, interrupting society's programmed functions and forms, they invite the autonomous and creative potential of each life to encounter and be put into play with the potential of other lives beyond the reach of society's networked capture.

107.

Each time lives manage to break out of the integrated separation of their coded identities and functional roles, they find themselves and one another in a situation that has not been reduced to its informatic and communicative form. This play of noncoded relations between lives and the expression of noncoded forms of life within a revolt allows lives not only to escape and confront domination together but also to take joy in the discovery and elaboration of what can only be done collectively and in common with other lives. Just as starling murmurations allow each bird to glide atop the turbulence generated by the wings of others, setting into motion many distinct currents that coalesce into an uncontrolled yet irreducibly shared atmosphere, revolts can be understood as the collective expression of many diverse potentials that culminates in a common potential that is qualitatively distinct from the sum of its calculated parts.

108.

If the reticular society aspires to code every possible permutation of *what life can be*, revolts are necessarily oriented instead toward the collective experimentation with *what life can potentially become*. The creative autonomy of life thus not only arises as essential to every struggle against domination—emerging as an insurgent disorder against society's recursively imposed order—but also is essentially what each of these struggles is *fought for*. Revolts can be understood as the militant actualization of potentials that cannot be coded, captured, computed, or contained, of potentials that are immanent to each life as well as shared and cultivated between lives. In the tumult of these ungovernable situations where dams of codes and data collapse and break apart in the flood of *something truly different*, where potentials break through what was calculated as possible, the oldest of friends can encounter one another anew, *as if for the first time*.

VII

Recognizing Domination

109.

The totality of the reticular society's informatic division and online capture culminates in a culture of recognition in which things come to be identified and perceived only as they have already been represented as data, in a culture of recognition that only experiences society as it has already been disintegrated into digital objects and reintegrated within the circulation of networks. In the flowing separations of online life, media is detonated into smaller and smaller pieces of content, life is exposed to denser and denser bursts of stimuli, and communication is cut into shorter and shorter strings of signifiers, collapsing our experience of the world into ever more fragmented and transient forms. In the culture of recognition, where every form of expression is steadily subsumed within and subordinated to a networked economy and exchange of the recognizable, lived reality disintegrates into atomized streams of accelerating content that aim to accumulate views and nothing more. Museums design their exhibitions to multiply opportunities for selfies, films are edited in anticipation of being sliced into memorable GIFs, songs are formulaically shortened to maximize streams, and AI platforms are prompted to generate a thousand minor variations of a dictator's portrait. As culture becomes ever more exclusively composed of ever more recognizable elements, culture functions to *stimulate attention and suppress contemplation*, to *simulate the experience of thinking* while *programmatically subduing thought itself.*

110.

Just as a computer can only load what is already encoded in its memory, in the reticular society the separation of contemplation into an algorithmic flutter of recognitions is designed to recursively establish the unified disunity of network perception, ideation, and representation, where what is viewed, touched, scanned, remembered, tapped, uploaded, imagined, and thought about any particular thing all *programmatically converge and become increasingly identical to one another online*. The storm felt soaking through a jacket becomes indistinguishable from the storm seen raining down on a crowd, which becomes indistinguishable from the storm measured by a smart city's sensors, which becomes indistinguishable from the storm's path modeled on screens, which becomes indistinguishable from the storm blowing through a dream. The unity of any particular object, the unity that arises among a life's sensation, perception, memory, imagination, and thought, which allows a life to recognize an object as an object, is in the reticular society always a unity *premised on and produced by the informatic disunity that governs it*. As each dimension of life comes to be mediated by data that is ever more detached from lived reality, as what is circulated and computed codes over every other possible experience, life comes to recognize the world only as the growing accumulation of its informatic fragmentation.

111.

In the reticular society's culture of recognition, lives perceive an endless flow of ever more discrete objects and thus become increasingly less able to contemplate the totality from which they emerge. The experience of totality, the lived experience of what intimately structures and suffuses all of life, is continuously interrupted by the separated experiences of society's totalized online disintegration. Politics and economics are grasped as a series of streamed debates and buzzworthy memes and thus are not experienced as the police installing a new surveillance post next to a public housing block or as a hospital turning the sick away because its budget has been slashed. Climate change and ecological collapse are grasped as a series of animated graphs and 3D models and thus are not experienced as the extinction of a butterfly or as the nearby river that has gone dry. Wars and conflicts are grasped as a series of filtered soldier selfies and flag icons placed on top of profile pictures and thus are not experienced as the expansion of refugee camps or the militarization of everyday life. If these things were fully experienced, if the violence of the present totality were *truly thought*, society would not be able to survive the revolts that would arrive as the only sensible response. Suppressing and subsuming the experience of society's total devastation online by separating it into a stream of detached data thus emerges as one of the reticular society's principal means of survival. Networks circulate so as to dissimulate the ruination they everywhere pursue.

112.

The cultural and informatic disintegration of lived experience ultimately causes the ever more numerous crises rippling across the planet—ecological, financial, political, atmospheric, existential—to appear as a multiplying accumulation of separated phenomena rather than as the historical expressions of a social totality, and thus each appear to require only their own discrete technical solutions, their own minor adjustments as isolated variables of society's unified calculation. As things become increasingly intelligible as detached things on networks, as they *appear as they circulate* and *circulate as they appear*, as lived reality comes not to be contemplated but sorted and scrolled through as a streaming series of separated objects online, any concept of history or totality sinks into the recesses of what society remains unable to think.

113.

The informatic objectification of the reticular society produces a culture in which decipherability precludes polysemy, where transparency precludes opacity, and where recognizability precludes intelligibility. Far-right political parties that circulate and consolidate coded conspiracies and objectifying slurs, liberal social media pages that periodically reshare the same collections of recycled slogans and solidarity emojis, and anonymous online message boards that repetitively shuffle through minor variations of the same misogynist punch lines and white supremacist memes are all expressions of a culture that is structured as a networked totality of recognition, of a culture in which recognizing objects reaffirms and intensifies already held ideas just as already held ideas about particular objects renders them ever more effortlessly recognizable as such. These online cycles of recognition are perhaps most clearly on display in the endless parade of superhero films, shows, and video games that combinatorially reshuffle through their recognizable sets of canonical references, crossover plots, and celebrity cameos, an increasingly automated aestheticization of politics that is recursively realized as the computer-rendered breasts and biceps of their manifestly fascist protagonists. In each instance, recognition assumes a centrality in the reticular society because it is *literally a re-cognizing*, a perceptual experience that is dominated by *a repetitive thinking of what has already been thought* and *revalidation of what was already represented as true*.

114.

The pleasure of recognition in the reticular society is the pleasure of a symmetry that is communicatively sustained between the exterior world and interior life, in which every time something is recognized it leads directly to a rediscovery and reaffirmation of already held assumptions, beliefs, and ideas about that thing. Like a student who has diligently memorized their professor's lectures and excitedly sits down to rephrase them for an online exam, a supermarket self-checkout terminal that algorithmically matches objects in a cart with objects in its price database, an airport security guard who listlessly scans their eyes back and forth over their screens looking to catch this or that prohibited water bottle or piece of fruit, a smartphone's capacitive sensor that programmatically searches for a correspondence between a fingerprint and a stored geometry of lines and curves, or a bored subway commuter swiping through a feed of remixed clips of an awards ceremony, recognition is entirely structured by the already known, familiar, exposed, identified, explained, and coded. Networked society strives to establish *an ever more total symmetry between a world recognized and a world represented as data*, suppressing all efforts to contemplate any inconsistency, discrepancy, or fissure between lived reality and its informatic abstraction.

115.

Each experience of recognition involves recursively traversing already enciphered circuits of perceptions and ideas in multiple directions. An edited video of a group of hooded teens seen on an online platform cascades into a recognition of delinquents or dropouts, which connects to ideas of poverty and domesticity, which further connects to ideas of Blackness and the inner city before returning back to further intensify the networked significations of the recognized form. An algorithm designed to recognize and detect faces at a passport kiosk, aiming to match skin tones, scars, irises, and lips with this criminal profile or that worker visa, is technically mirrored in a life that recognizes and remembers the scripted gestures expected by the kiosk, brushes their hair aside, poses, and smiles into the screen's camera. A captioned photo of a woman wearing a hijab on a subway prompts a recognition of a victim or a suspect, which connects to ideas of gender and coloniality, which further connects to ideas of sexuality and war before mapping back onto the recognition again. A tourist driving out to visit a settlement in an occupied territory puts on their smart glasses and sees the nearby fields, villages, olive trees, and security checkpoints digitally highlighted and labeled, recognizing an unfamiliar world in an informatically familiar way. Across infinite variations of these repetitive series effectuated by lives and machines alike, *already held ideas flood through perceptions just as perceptions themselves fold back to further consolidate and recirculate already held ideas.*

116.

An entirely recognized and represented society is ultimately a society in which nothing unexpected or surprising takes place, a society in which experience itself has come to be objectified, a society in which everything is thought and found precisely how it always already was, how it apparently is, and how it will indefinitely continue to be. A generalized amnesia structures the entire experience of society, in which everything appears dazzlingly new and thus without history, consequence, or cause. Like the online streaming services that seamlessly transition between episodes so that subscribers never have to look away or ponder what to view next, the subsumption of all lived experience within online modes of recognition is algorithmically oriented toward the perpetual deadening and deferral of thought. It is less *aesthetic* than it is *anesthetic*, not aiming to affect life but to let life slip away into the desensitized, neutralized, and pacified comforts of an online existence, endlessly deferring any possible conflict by drawing it within the circulation of the already familiar and known.

117.

When stuck in a mode of recognition, experience is structured wholly by what has already been recognized and represented and thus by what has already been made to be socially recognizable, allowing life to live in the world without having to truly encounter or contemplate anything at all. The most banal violence of the culture of recognition can be located in the experience of an online life in which all of social reality has been flattened out and made equivalent, in which the most desolating and most quotidian things can be clicked through inconsequentially and just the same. Top ten lists of celebrity fashion disasters and summer pop hits circulate online alongside the top ten ways to avoid having your bathroom visits digitally tracked at work, the top ten glaciers you have to see before they disappear forever, the top ten ways to become an alpha male and dominate women on the dating scene, and the top ten most brutal police executions filmed this year. Oil futures for sale on an investing app, a video clip of a brawl between a fascist gang and a group of refugees, and a former soldier hosting virtual classes for military contractors about how to survive and thrive in conflict zones are each seen only as the online sum of their disintegrated data, and thus they occlude the material and historical conditions that sustain and compose them, ensuring they can continue to be endlessly consumed without any consideration. Expansive swaths of the earth turn arid and barren, life is brutalized and impoverished, and networks circulate smoothly just the same.

118.

The reticular society's culture of recognition extends so totally that even the most extreme forms of devastation aren't discarded or disowned but rather are recuperated and recycled as digital objects to further populate and propel network circulation. Short, looping clips of floodwaters washing over entire towns, politicians making racist gaffes, gender reveal parties sparking vast wildfires, armed police officers patrolling primary schools, mass shooting sprees at mosques and synagogues, soldiers throwing grenades into trenches, climate activists being pepper-sprayed on highways, and endangered species building nests of discarded electronics are all packaged and flow across networks as recognizable data, joining endless streams of fragmented novelty that are optimized to draw all attention but that culminate only in a banal and bored monotony that reflects the homogeneity of their underlying form. Just as snowflakes melt and vanish into the sea, *even the most ruinous expressions of the reticular society are smoothly liquidated* in the programmed circulation of what they move through.

119.

Atomized instances of recognition culminate into a generalized culture of recognition in the reticular society across two dimensions, first in networked machines that represent and recognize society as data, and second in lives that perceive society as networked machines already have and thus ultimately come to perceive networks as society. The mode of recognition that structures all forms of perception in networked life, typified in the activity of visually scanning through fragmented pieces of content on platforms and feeds that prompt repetitive moments of recognition, resembles and is tightly coupled with the cars outfitted with advanced camera rigs that now drive through the world's urban centers in order to capture street imagery for digital maps, detecting and tagging traffic signs, faces, logos, storefronts, trash, monuments, and advertisements along the way. Networked life, recognition, and representation here converge entirely in the experience of the pedestrian who prefers to look at the lists of walking directions, recommended shops, weather reports, and social ratings displayed on the smartphone in their hand rather than the surrounding world, inevitably bumping into and colliding with other lives and things but remaining intimately in sync with the data flowing through the air around them. When something unexpected does actually happen at school, on the street, or at work, it has become easiest to simply recognize it as something being staged and filmed for online circulation as the world itself comes to appear intuitively as a set for the production of content to be uploaded to and shared on platforms. Online and on phones, in surveillance footage and in selfies, on sidewalks and on hikes, the culture of recognition *imposes itself as an experiential totality*, foreclosing the possibility that society could be sensed, encountered, or experienced in a way that differs in any meaningful sense from the way it already circulates informatically.

120.

The represented and recognized accumulation of society's objective fragmentation culminates in a culture that can only recognize and only seeks recognition, in a vast stream of informatic objects that serves as the cultural means of *dominating thought itself as another object*. What has been called the attention economy is better described as a networked economy of recognition, an economy within which contemplation has come to be subsumed and subordinated. Each life comes to experience society as an ever more personalized stream of objects that has been algorithmically adjusted to be more and more recognizable to them in particular, just as the aggregate data collected about lives recognizing these and those things is used to reprogram and optimize the totality of culture. Culture thus works to keep society's attention moving along and in the process learns to more optimally target the attention of particular lives, just as the attention of particular lives is the analytical basis for more optimally moving society's attention along collectively. The stream and the feed are weaponized against particular lives, while the platform and the interface are correspondingly optimized as a weapon against life in general. The separation of the world into recognizable objects and the corresponding separation of contemplation into recognitions in the end works to produce *an objectified consciousness that circulates online as if it were also simply another piece of data*, digitally tethered to the fragments of content designed to drag all thought along with them.

121.

As networked activity deepens the culture of recognition and thus deepens the intellectual passivity of whatever connects, life steadily comes to be spent *thinking less and less about more and more things*. Any capacity to perceive the world with others, to collectively grasp what is common and shared in a situation, splinters and bursts into flows of fragmented objects that further fragment society in turn. Each life *sees their own particular stream of data as the world*, just as the integration of all attention into the feed causes lives to *share only the algorithmic disintegration of their experience in common*. Networks aspire to have everything move in a fundamentally controlled way online, as ceaseless as it is atomized, so that minds wander less and less. The algorithmic flow of recognizable objects online is ultimately oriented toward the cancellation of contemplation, just as the supposed intelligence of machine learning models and smart devices is reflected socially only in the generalized stupidity they induce. Submerged within society's protocolic depths, the circulation of thought on networks leaves *only what circulates on networks thinkable*.

122.

While it is immensely difficult to disconnect from society's networks, it is strikingly easy to emotionally and ethically detach oneself from what flows across them. Just as residents of a metropolis steadily become accustomed to strolling by those who sleep on the street, on networks lives steadily become accustomed to scrolling by the desolation of life on feeds, remaining essentially unmoved by the violence that moves so voluminously online. Lives consume ever more accelerated streams of content that display the suffering and pain of the world, their form more stimulating as their content grows more horrific, and yet the accumulation of this consumption only deepens life's generalized indifference and paralysis. Every time a life becomes simply another separated spectator of society's desolation, every time a life is further immersed in isolated streams that steadily deliver society's devastation as a cascade of discrete digital objects, *they too are deadened in the process*, literally becoming less alive as they scroll through feeds but do not feel, as they respond with likes and comments but at the expense of any other possible response. Nowhere is this more apparent than in the repeated mass drownings of migrants that are captured in immense detail by advanced security technologies and then uploaded to networks, but that circulate only to convince online audiences that the catastrophe is already underway and that clicking "reshare" is all that can be done. Within this online undertow that often escapes notice but never ceases to drag life into its numbing depths, *lives increasingly recognize the degree to which society's desolation expands* just as they become *increasingly immobilized by and indifferent to it.*

123.

The alienation and detachment that flow everywhere throughout the reticular society are subjectively expressed in forms of networked spectatorship that further subordinate the world to its online circulation. Society comes to appear as something that is not only *to be passively seen* but also as something *to be actively streamed*, in which the automated velocity of networks is negatively mirrored in the relative stillness of those who capture and upload videos to them. Even in moments of naked and unrestrained violence—a trans musician being targeted and attacked at a club, a security guard putting a teenager in a chokehold beside a pool, city workers destroying the tents of an informal encampment, riot police beating striking workers at a smartphone factory—those who are nearby and in a position to do something very rarely intervene but are always more than ready to pull out their phones. Like the backpackers in pristine mountain resorts who point their cell phones up toward nearby peaks to capture clips of the avalanches that rapidly approach to bury them, *the digital recognition, representation, and circulation of the world appears as more real and urgent than the world itself.* This networked spectatorship is on full display in those moments when revolt periodically does openly confront power in the streets, where each brick thrown is exceedingly outnumbered by the dozens of cameras that snap photos of and stream its flight through the air. The reticular society is the nightmare of a society that stares into its own abyss and can only think to press stream and record.

124.

The culture of recognition in the reticular society is everywhere built on and extends the forms of representation and recognition that historically have structured all capitalist social relations. Under capitalism, a life can walk down the street and literally perceive in each thing and in each other life a price. A bird gliding overhead, a bus stop displaying an advertisement, a sanitation worker hauling trash bags to their truck, a piece of graffiti sprayed onto a brick wall, and a song playing through wireless headphones can each be grasped as an amount of money and mediated on that basis. Lives come to subjectively relate to the world principally on the basis of its abstraction as the world itself comes to be recognized only as a collection of objects whose value is determined by their perceived position in the capitalist regime of value, permitting themselves to carve their names deeply into trees but keeping a safe distance from sports cars less they accidentally smudge them, to verbally abuse the baristas taking their orders but politely defer to the clerks reviewing their loan applications, to carefully care for their laptops but carelessly waste the water that is used to cool their cryptocurrency mining rigs. This mode of perception is so total that investors can even virtually extend it into their imaginations, seeing prices and profits in things that have yet to exist.

125.

The capacity to experience the world solely as a set of objectified commodities and abstract prices under capitalism is further developed in the reticular society as the ability to perceive in each thing, and in each life, data. A walk is seen as an object of gait analysis and calories burned, a face a surface for the capture of micro expressions and algorithmically generated makeup suggestions, a drop of blood a genetic sample for a criminal database or the prediction of a child's future financial and social success, and a dead coral reef a chance to post a clip online and gain a subscriber or two. Looking around over the course of a day, data appears to pour forth from every crevice, as a spare bedroom appears as a chance to list it online for short-term rental, a pair of shoes delivered to a doorstep appears as a chance to stream an unboxing video, and the interior of a refrigerator appears as a chance to snap and upload a photo to an AI platform that can suggest recipes for dinner. In an opposite yet symmetrical dimension, things also come to appear as essentially imbued with data from elsewhere, as a smart thermostat in a living room, an e-bike parked on a street, and a smart storage locker at a train station all depend on data streamed from networks to function at all. The density of these recognitions and representations ultimately emerges as a society that is experienced in such high resolution that its informatic form feels more real than reality, but whose common denominator remains the unreality of networks. The datafication and circulation of lived reality is so thorough that if something doesn't exist online, if it hasn't been captured and multiplied and made accessible across many networked forms, it's easy to assume that it may not exist at all. Grasping reality first as data follows from the generalized intuition that reality exists only as *a shadow of its online form*, alienating life from everything but the integrated separation of its networked abstraction.

126.

Periodic encounters with the unrecognizable can emerge in the reticular society's culture of recognition, but whenever the unrecognizable does appear it does so only in the form of social ruptures that fundamentally disturb and disrupt lives' ability to recognize themselves and the world and that thus appear as deeply hostile and alien forces. Constituted by what Frantz Fanon wrote of as the circuits of recognition that formalize and sustain relations of domination, the culture of recognition that thrives in the reticular society responds to the appearance of the unrecognizable either by attempting to capture, subsume, and recuperate the unrecognized thing as a new additional entry in its datasets and thus expand its represented and recognized online reality, or by moving to eradicate and expunge that thing as a pernicious glitch or anomaly or error in an otherwise uniform, transparent, and predictable system. In the reticular society, it is unsurprising that queer, undocumented, sick, incarcerated, unemployed, and disabled lives, those lives that remain to some degree unrecognizable and unrepresentable because they resist being frictionlessly and uniformly integrated into society, generate so much paranoia and scrutiny, ultimately appearing socially only as broken objects in need of repair or, alternatively, disposal. Trans lives are paradigmatic in this regard precisely because of the problems they pose for recognition, at once being treated as objects to be carefully investigated, assessed, and examined and as objects to be violently purged, deleted, and expelled. In the reticular society, when the unrecognizable does appear, it does so as nothing less than a vertiginous fissure running through the entire foundation of the recognized and represented world, a crack in the process of recognition that threatens to swallow the unified representation of the world whole.

127.

Adjacent to the hostile suppression of the unrecognizable, a life's failure to be recognized as data in the reticular society also has the effect of canceling and negating their social existence. For a life that misplaced their login or password and gets locked out of a medical system's scheduling software after too many incorrect attempts, or for a life whose face cannot be algorithmically matched with an image in a database and gets denied passage through an automated checkpoint, the success or failure to represent and recognize life as data converges entirely with a life's ability to survive within society or be left behind by it. Within these circuits of recognition, life comes to be lived between two extreme poles: It either experiences the world as a smooth integration where everything appears to work together automatically and effortlessly, or it experiences the world as an unresponsive grid of locked barriers, error messages, gated services, circulating rejections, and automated exclusions. The violence of being recognized and represented online is everywhere structured and sustained by a parallel violence that arrives when a life fails to be recognized and represented and is excluded and abandoned on those terms.

128.

Among the most advanced technologies of the culture of recognition are the machine learning models trained on data scraped from the internet that produce new representations in automated fashions. Having been set to recognize the patterns found in books, articles, posts, poems, and forums, chatbots generate new texts that statistically conform to the prior word sequences that had been integrated into their model's architectures. Other models trained on collections of images produce novel visuals based on the formal and aesthetic qualities of the data they have subsumed, reproducing the curve of a hip or the deep green hues of the sea according to their coded parameters. Models can be used to write grocery lists, suggest interior design strategies, and draft college essays just as they can be used to generate counterinsurgency tactics, produce propaganda about subjugated groups, and schedule oil-drilling projects. These technologies produce unique outputs, but what is unique is only the probabilistic expression of what had already been formally recognized and represented as data within them. In these systems, a *past fragmented into bits and bytes computationally folds into fragmented futures*, closely resembling the forms that preceded them in every meaningful way. Machine learning and its adjacent technologies thus represent the culture of recognition in perhaps its most distilled form, simply repeating what has already been articulated and visualized, compelling society to submit to the *technically inexhaustible representation and recognition of what was already represented and recognized in society*. Culture devolves into the infinite accumulation of similarity, into the automated reproduction of a symmetry between what already was and what is made to appear as new.

129.

The reticular society's perpetual accumulation of informatic objects ultimately produces forms of recognition and representation that are wholly uncoupled and freed from the world itself. As data comes to represent the world at ever higher degrees of informatic resolution and as image and language models are trained on that data, new representations can be generated not by referencing the world but by drawing on the data that has already been abstracted. Just as capital always advances and returns as its own accumulation, what begins as a reticulated loop between life and data is only the preliminary stage of a historical movement that steadily detaches as its own separate reality. In a world where everything atrophies except for information and circulation, the totality of the reticular society is oriented not toward the universal but the *metaversal*, a technical destiny where society comes to be composed not of representations of the world but only of *representations of representations*, of *investments in investments*, of *screenshots of screenshots*, of *data about data*. This liberation of digital information from its signifying function allows it to proceed as its own autonomous force, as an undead circulation that flows against the living. Aspiring to fully realize itself as *the unrestrained automation of simulation*, a society that captures lives as data hungers to consume life once and for all, dreaming of an enciphered vacuum where a perfectly abstract structure has been liberated from all of lived reality, where there are only machines communicating with machines and there is nothing left to recognize, represent, or reference except for *the dead space of its own reticulated reality.*

VIII

Graphing Insurgency

130.

The domination of the reticular society always has a tendency to further abstract itself, ultimately aiming not only to subordinate networked lives but also to grasp and dominate life itself, as if it too were simply a network. This formal development culminates in a society within which lives relate to one another on networked terms, but also in a society whose relations are so communicatively and informatically subsumed that acting on the network form comes to take precedence over acting on whatever is discretely connected to it. At this higher degree of abstraction, an abstraction that is formalized as *the online relation of relations*, the reticular society realizes itself not simply as a continuation of capitalist world history but as *a novel form of domination within it*.

131.

The shift from the networked domination of life to the domination of life as a network is realized historically in the technology of the graph. Building on the human terrain systems that were developed and deployed against Southeast Asian and Black insurgencies in the late twentieth century, graphs diagram life as a mesh of nodes and links in order to formally expand the operation of power beyond the individual, understood as a part, as well as beyond the population, understood as a whole, so that domination can act on the dynamic relation of relations that compose network geometries. The graph takes the network form as a strategic space, allowing domination to strengthen and consolidate sections of a network that are identified as productive and useful and to weaken and starve inefficient or disobedient formations. Communicative flows between consumers, politicians, corporations, influencers, engineers, and police are all multiplied and intensified, while those between prisoners, migrants, dissidents, and the unemployed are impeded and dispersed in hopes of rerouting them into more profitable circuits and channels. The graph weaponizes geometry itself as part of the execution of domination, escaping the need to act on or police this or that life identified solely as an isolated individual or node and instead allowing networks to act on the links, densities, clusters, and intensities that structure network activity. In other words, the graph is what allows *the form and content of domination to technically coincide*. The graph is *domination reticulated.*

132.

In the geopolitical conflicts, counterinsurgency operations, and colonial occupations that have populated the early twenty-first century, forces of domination have put to use a novel repertoire of strategies and tactics based on the graph form. One way this embrace of the graph was first expressed was in the embedding of anthropologists with combat units in Afghanistan. The anthropologists collected biometric information about and conducted interviews with the lives that populated the subjugated terrain, data that then was used to *translate life itself into a tactical environment* that could be modeled, simulated, and acted on as a network. Equipped with the graph form, military strategists could target unruly and insurgent sections of a network geometry—infiltrating, subduing, or eliminating those sets and clusters of links as a means of demobilizing or disabling the disobedient sections of a graph—just as they could provide resources to other subsets of networked relations in order to centralize and bolster the network structure around those areas that conformed and complied most neatly with the military's imposed order. The ideal form of the reticular society arises not as a map that statically delineates friendly and enemy territories, nor as a grid that strictly assigns lives across its coded cells and axes, but as a graph that responsively diagrams and modifies the relation of relations between networked lives.

133.

As part of the recursive policification of militaries and militarization of police forces, the shift toward a reticulated execution of domination premised on the graph has additionally come to be expressed in domestic forms of repression that leverage the network form as the basis for experimental executions of control. In several of the major insurrections of the most recent decades, regimes have opted to not send in police to violently clear the streets but have instead sent text messages to those in the vicinity of the disorder, warning that they have been recorded as present in a zone of social unrest and that they must disperse and leave the area immediately. This hostile communication directed toward lives that have been graphed as part of concentrated clusters of undesired network activity acts on them subjectively and objectively, intending to identify and terrorize them as the surveilled and disciplined subjects of a violent regime while also capturing and recording them as informatic objects of a city graphed as a network. However, the effect of dominating particular lives remains secondary and subordinated to the true function of this type of repression: to reconfigure the larger network geometry into *a less hostile and volatile one*, dispersing antagonism into a less dense and less intense distribution and thus *diminishing its potential to proliferate disorder within or punch holes through the network form*.

134.

The networked repression and domination of life as a graph has also taken shape in the increasing regularity of preemptive arrests executed in advance of anticipated periods of revolt, in which authorities identify densely linked and highly active clusters of nodes to detain and isolate on the network before things really kick off, aspiring to douse revolts in advance of their ignition. While the attacks are executed on groups of singular nodes, their intended effect is directed at the network geometry as a whole, aiming not to terrorize particular lives but to *circulate terror across the broader flows of an uprising*. Networked lives exist both as *nodes that are subjected to operations of power* and *as relays through which power passes*, finding themselves exposed to despotic forms of violence just as they are subsumed within the violent circulations of the network form. This form of directed repression executed within the geometry of the graph has also at times been coupled with the juridical designation of protest zones, delimited territories that are outfitted with security barriers and advanced surveillance technologies that invite revolts to take place, but on the network's chosen terrain. Both of these modes of repression and domination don't aim to preclude or extinguish revolt but rather move to remold and reshape it as a graph as a means of dispersing its force, lowering its intensity, and folding it back into a recuperated and manageable online form.

135.

The domination of the graph aspires to impose a symmetry on all forms of insurgency and revolt, to capture even those who desire to annihilate networked society within networked flows and forms. By preemptively imposing its own graphed order on predicted waves of disorder, online forms of domination aim to allow revolts to take place in a way that will allow them to expend and expose themselves but not escape the society they confront. In each instance, networked society aspires to steer revolts into a confrontation with a reticulated reflection, in which they can be repressed and recuperated precisely because their insurgent energies have come to be mirrored, monitored, and modulated online. The graph here arises as the formal and technical expression of the fantasy that broadly gives shape to the execution of domination in the reticular society, a fantasy that Jasbir Puar has described as the dream that resistance itself can be wholly subsumed computationally by power, that resistance can be entirely located, emptied, and subjugated by networks that seek to effectively capture and compute revolt as a digital object. Whatever forces emerge against networked society inevitably find themselves confronting technologies of domination that dream of frictionlessly subsuming and subduing them within the geometries and symmetries of the network form.

136.

Anything can potentially be graphed as a network as a question of technical and formal method. Graphs can be strung across the squares of chess boards or the inputs and outputs of cybernetic systems, linked to the intersections of neighborhood maps or the characters moving through the narratives of science fiction novels, tethered to a group of university students or to an ant colony or to the players of an online game or to boxes stacked at a port or to the families of a migrant caravan. Even given this high degree of formal mobility and flexibility, a society already organized as a network lends itself to being graphed and acted on as a network in far more optimal and effective ways, allowing for the difference between the graph and the territory to effectively vanish as they bleed into each other's isomorphic shadows. Graphs thus do not function to statically map a social world that has been entirely fixed but rather to *affix the social world to a graph that allows it to be transformed as the graph is*. As with all of the technologies of the reticular society, there is little to be gained from distinguishing between the graph's subsumption and subjugation of life. In a tight technological loop between informatic capture and circulating control, *graphing and acting on life as a network* has the effect of *producing more intensely networked lives*, just as lives that come to be further networked are more exposed to network domination.

137.

The digitized devastation of contemporary warfare now fully expresses the logic of the graph in its execution, ever more closely aligning online geometries with the obliteration of life. In Israel's genocidal assault on Gaza, a networked resemblance between what is tracked as information and what is technologically annihilated is sustained as a means of sustaining the total scope of Israel's colonial violence. Lives, devices, vehicles, and architectures are all subsumed as data and integrated into a graph of the field of operations, and are then bombarded and shot at to effectuate reorganizations of the graph's geometry as part of the military's mass slaughter and total carnage. Israeli-controlled communication infrastructures are kept online to keep Gazans connected, but only so they can remain informatically integrated within the state's circulating violence and be analyzed by AI technologies that select them for elimination. Missiles are rained down across whole neighborhoods in order to kill, but also to send people fleeing south so they will have to pass through biometric checkpoints and be further integrated into the online machines of death. Maps of Gaza that have been subdivided into numbered subsections are uploaded and shared online and then are used to execute rearrangements and redistributions of the graphed form by ordering lives to flee particular areas and relocate to others, calibrating the war zone so as to optimize a decimating violence. Within the militarized segments of networked geometries, the online graph subsumes life only to further exterminate it.

138.

When the reticular society aspires to graph reality, it also aspires to graph history, aiming to align all past, present, and future activities with the activity of the networks that have been cast over them. The graph is a technology characterized not only by a total surveillance of the present, in which each thing, gesture, and relation is diagrammed and circulated as data as part of an ever more complex and total network geometry, but also by an ever-expanding matrix of predictions that are computationally based on analyses of past data and extend into the future. The graph thus aspires to diagram each and every thing a particular life has done as well as the different future branches of what that life might possibly do, a procedure that then is repeated across all of the lives integrated into a network geometry. This form of analysis is ultimately implemented with the aim of producing programmed futures that remain formally symmetrical to surveilled pasts, taking shape as a densely represented history projected into an eminently recognizable future.

139.

In the coded capture of historical time, new technologies appear to blink to life everywhere and interfaces and platforms are persistently updated, but they function only to ensure that life remains perpetually stuck in the same accelerating rhythms of work, debt, policing, surveillance, war, and rising sea levels. The graph can thus be thought of as a technology that dominates the order of the world but also the order of time, seeking to dominate not just life but *also its past and future*. The networked colonization of time doesn't aspire only to defuse and defang the past and future, but also to recuperate them as data and thus transform them into additional algorithmic resources for society's accumulative progress, subsuming them within a circulating uniformity that aspires to flow uninterrupted in perpetuity. Within these reticulated operations that cast webs across space and time, the relations of the Paris Commune are modeled by digital humanities labs just as venture capitalists pour investments into AI projects that devastate lives in the present for the imagined benefit of future lives. Past military battles are translated into data and then modeled as algorithmic simulations that can be replayed like games, allowing armies to search for more optimized outcomes and develop strategies for conflicts to come, not even letting the dead or the unborn escape society's networked grasp.

140.

Whenever lives do come to desire their own autonomy and thus desire to revolt—as all life has the spontaneous and ineradicable potential to do when dominated—networks aspire to give them expression while ensuring society's networked relations remain fundamentally uninterrupted and unchallenged. The reticular society understands that so long as revolts *remain connected to what has connected them as separate*, and thus remain captured within and dependent on the very things that dominate them, they will remain as nothing more than a minor error to be eliminated, as a passing expression of a networked imbalance that can inevitably be resolved within society's networked progress. Everything in the reticular society has the tendency to begin online simply because it is expressed within a totality that is formalized as the networked subsumption of all things, and as a result even those revolts that are directed most intensely against networked society have often first been sparked and catalyzed by a video circulating online or a call posted on a platform. The principal task of every uprising is thus to take what was found online and expand and intensify the struggle beyond and against the networked capture that strives to determine its form, to *tear open an insurgent time and space within society's online geometry of nodes and links*, to break away from the diagrammatic reach of the graph and bring the emergent conflicts and struggles ever further offline.

141.

In truly insurrectionary situations where the survivability of particular regimes has been violently called into question, those with their hands on the consoles of power no longer find themselves tempted to shut off the internet but rather have learned that it's far more preferable to keep everyone connected, continuing to capture them within networked relations that can surveil, subsume, and eventually subdue them. While it is still possible to occasionally see this or that outmoded regime try to cut off access during periods of unrest, the more advanced sectors of the reticular society know that it is not networked censorship or silence but rather the intensification and multiplication of society's networked communication that best neutralizes disorder. Domination does not aspire to eliminate this or that part of a network that would only compromise and contract the totality of the network form but rather sets out to effectuate changes in a network graph's geometry over time—weakening particular links while strengthening others, scattering a cluster of nodes over there and concentrating another cluster here, accelerating these flows and slowing those—in order to modulate and reshape the overall activity and output of networked life toward more optimized ends. The graph functions both extensively and intensively, striving to *remake the geometric relation between the elements of a network* in order to *modulate the potentialities that can be expressed across it*. This is recuperation at its most refined, providing revolt with a network form so that even the most boundless chaos arises as another opportunity to further connect, reroute, capture, optimize, and steer things in this or that desired direction.

142.

The smartphone is the technology that perhaps represents the purest and densest crystallization of the reticular society, formally unifying the graph, the enciphering and deciphering of life, and the connected separation that suffuses all social relations. Never in history has so much of life been tracked, encoded, and compressed into a single object, into a single apparatus, into a single device, its screen a glossy chasm that swallows and regurgitates each of society's dimensions in informatic, networked, and alienated forms. Smartphones guide traffic, transcribe speech, generate schedules, record images and videos, share locations, scan fingerprints and faces, transfer funds, stream games, log in to work, confess to the authorities, translate signs, take out loans, store IDs, make calls, and transmit orders. They are bombed by drones, surveilled during pandemics, targeted for ads by politicians, scanned at airport terminals, and hacked by intelligence agencies. Friends buy movie tickets to cool off inside during a heat wave, and when they pay with their smartphones, they send packets of information to data centers on the other side of the world that are kept online by burning fossil fuels and firing union organizers. Professional streamers perform on the otherwise abandoned sidewalks of wealthy neighborhoods in hopes that their smartphones will be geolocated closer to and thus attract higher-paying online audiences. In the smartphone we see the totality of the reticular society most clearly objectified, an objectification that is so total that the networked domination of life has come to be increasingly synonymous with the networked domination of life's devices.

143.

The smartphone is a paradigmatic apparatus of the reticular society because of the way in which it innovates on the fundamentally binary apparatuses that preceded it. In subway turnstiles that sort lives into paying commuters and criminal fare evaders, in border checkpoints that parse populations into wealthy tourists and undocumented migrants, or in fingerprint scanners that distinguish between the hands of docile citizens and hunted terrorists, we see apparatuses that split life into classes of this and that form of life, a form of binary division and domination that reduces lives to this or that positive or negative, major or minor term. The strategic function of the apparatus is to impose binary relations between diverse elements, to capture all life together and then code lives apart, or, as Tiqqun articulated, to establish *polarized spaces that reduce everything that passes through them to one or the other of its terms*. The apparatus is fundamentally premised on the digital logic of circulation and partition, sieving and sorting life in order to subsequently dominate differentiated lives, allowing individuals to *flow everywhere as binary variables of society's circulating separation*.

144.

Building on and further developing the binary apparatuses that so densely populate the history of capitalism, the reticular society captures lives not solely on the basis of their existence as individuals with this or that predicated identity, nor simply on the basis of their classes that are formalized on those binary terms, but additionally on the basis of their subsumption within a network geometry that is indifferent to any predicated identity. The reticular society arises not simply as an accumulation of apparatuses but rather as a network that links them together, concatenates them, flows across them, and initiates abstract operations based on their communicative unification. While the node of a network may still be identified by an apparatus and continue to be dominated on that basis—as a worker, thief, homosexual, communist, foreigner, anarchist, debtor—life also finds itself subjected to a form of reticulated domination that acts on lives based on *their relations within a graph*—as a pivotal bridge between two otherwise distant clusters, as part of a particular transformation or reconfiguration of nodes and links, as an outlier at a network's edge, as a component of a particular networked operation. Networked apparatuses code lives as *this or that binary class of life*, while the network itself functions as an *apparatus of apparatuses that imposes its geometric violence on all of social life*.

145.

The networking of apparatuses in the reticular society facilitates the forms of domination that are characteristic of both disciplinary and control power, homing in on subjective individuals and flowing across network geometries flexibly and as needed. Lives that speak multiple languages and link together linguistically distinct clusters of a network during a period of revolt, lives that introduce friction into the flows of networks and slow the productive activity of other lives connected to them, or lives that routinely break apart the dense collections of links that typify the consolidation of power on networks are all lives that may be subjected to various network operations in order to ensure the continuity and progress of the network's circulating domination. In the connected separation of networks, life is parsed ever more totally as identified and isolated lives just as it is dominated on the basis of its graphed relations within a network structure whose abstract geometry overshadows any individual actuality. Subsumed within online geometries, *who or what a life is* comes to be less formally significant for society's domination than *who or what a life is connected to*.

146.

Apparatuses such as the smartphone are integrated into the apparatus of the network so that the movement of workers can be graphed over time, allowing bosses and managers to detect anomalous concentrations and patterns and thus to preemptively identify and eliminate potential theft, sabotage, or union organizing. The daily routines and rhythms of undocumented communities are graphed and then used to render them increasingly vulnerable and thus increasingly exploitable by strategically deploying housing raids, ID checks, and control points. As cloud computing infrastructures spew vast amounts of carbon dioxide into the atmosphere and help intensify cycles of extreme droughts and violent storms, smartphones in cars and trucks reroute them around flooded areas and spreading wildfires to ensure that climate catastrophes don't slow down package deliveries or prevent anyone from getting to work on time. The density of smartphones in an office district is used to optimize the pricing of hailed car rides and maximize the extraction of profit across a network, and the movement of smartphones in a protest is used to redistribute squads of riot police to algorithmically selected intersections. The smartphone is in all of these ways both an apparatus and part of a network of apparatuses, facilitating a form of domination that surveils and imposes itself on individuals just as it is imposed at a higher level of abstraction on the networked relation of relations. It functions as a binary apparatus that operates on the basis of life's predicates and also moves beyond the individual and the population as a reticulated apparatus that grasps *the network itself as the space to be geometrically managed, controlled, and dominated.*

147.

In addition to serving as an apparatus as well as communicatively linking together many diverse apparatuses, the smartphone fulfills one more essential function in the reticular society by ensuring that *lives remain within reach of networks* and that *networks remain within reach of lives.* Even in those exceptional moments that pass disconnected, offline, and out of range—in a remote hike with friends across the Pyrenees, in an exclusive digital detox retreat on the central California coast, in the spotty reception of a bus trip across Cairo, in a flooded neighborhood of Beijing where cell towers have lost power—the smartphone collects information and stores what is needed from the network until it is able to reconnect, resituate, and resynchronize itself online again. While the world bears witness to an endless profusion of network technologies that seemingly aspire to link together reality in ever more refined resolutions and ubiquitous forms—from smartwatches to smart televisions, from networked bus stops to networked highway pavements, from police body cams to experimental military smart dust that blankets the surfaces of environments—the smartphone remains the apparatus that is most intimately integrated with and embraced by life.

148.

The sustained connection between lives and networks facilitated by smartphones is largely what possibilizes the perpetual choreography that is sustained between networks that are lived and lives that are networked. As this motion or that pose is undertaken with the smartphone in hand, gestures generate and drift away as data. Data also arrives to invite and instruct gestures, literally rewriting and rewiring the embodied vocabulary and grammar within which life is lived. The smartphone's formalization and scripting of the body is expressed not only in the subordination of the hand to the screen, transforming each of the hand's digits into yet another digital input for networks, but also in all of the faces that tilt down toward their respective devices, literally drawing lives to turn away from everything around them. Whether during concerts or while driving, when accompanying children to school or taking shelter during air raid sirens, at the park or in a restaurant, the same manual gestures and slouched poses reappear across bodies, reproducing and sustaining a resemblance across otherwise diverse lives. Across homogeneous interfaces and glossy screens, the smartphone choreographs the uniform gestures of networked life.

149.

All of the various social functions of smartphones are cumulatively the realization of the reticulated desolation that they objectively materialize. Smartphones are grasped as singular and discrete technical objects, yet they remain as assemblages that link together a global machine of toxic mines worked by child laborers, server farms sucking water away from drought-stricken regions, vast datasets labeled and sanitized by refugees, and venture capitalists who invest in these tech startups and those authoritarian think tanks. This objectification is so total that a life can hold a smartphone in their hand, this incredibly dense compression of planetary exploitation, violence, and alienation, and understand it as simply their own little object, as something they exclusively and separately possess, as the thing that allows them to individually express themselves, to take shelter in their own digital enclaves, to consume what they alone and privately wish, to be who they really are. All of the networks of fragmentation and domination that suffuse the production and use of smartphones are packed into the isolated experience of a device that contains a life's data, history, contacts, memories, and secrets, into an object that possibilizes and reproduces the connected separation of all social life. There are few things that can so clearly express the alienation that circulates through and is imposed on life in the reticular society, through which everything is tied together within totalizing webs of violent domination that relentlessly contract reality into the lived poverty of isolated forms.

IX

Horizons of Revolt

150.

Analyses of network society tend to cycle between feverish paranoia, accelerationist denial, and defeated resignation. In one moment, digital communication appears to be subsuming reality at such a rate that the future can be imagined only as an endless intensification of networked domination that life cannot ever possibly hope to outrun or defeat. In another, the reticular society's domination appears only as a passing defect that can be corrected for across the long arc of history, and thus the only task that presents itself is to further accelerate the development of networked social relations so that they can finally break free of the limits that constrain their potential. In still another, the networked colonization of life appears to already have been completed long ago and thus hums along as the technical background noise of the present society, offering lives only the possibility of accomplishing this or that minor reform that might subtly soften the violence that flows so profusely all around. All of these analyses are irreducibly thought within the language of the reticular society itself, within the circulating monologue that moves to coil together every beginning and end as well as loop together every entrance and exit, within the networked ontology that circulates the capture of all forms of being.

151.

The reticular society arises as the historical movement that aspires to suspend all movement but its own, as the circulating history that programmatically advances only the separated accumulation of its own domination. The more the reticular society interoperably enfolds all of life into its own perpetual unfolding, the more death informatically flows through all that lives. However, it is precisely because life is caught within this networked colonization that we know that life's autonomous and creative potential persists and is not exhausted, even if only captively and in the penumbras of society's domination, even if only as the very thing that networked society aims to totally capture, constrain, and crush. As the reticular society relentlessly encroaches on life, *revolt itself emerges as the power of life*, as a lived potential that cannot be wholly subsumed within or subordinated to society's networked domination. Life thus continues to be lived as the struggle to become ever more *incompatible with networked society*, to *short-circuit capitalism's forms and flows*, to abandon networked forms of life in search of what remains *asymmetrical and incommensurable*, to strike dissonant chords and *multiply into an insurgent cacophony of what remains living.*

152.

Life's insurgent potential stretches across horizons of revolt that can be glimpsed from within the networked totality that composes the reticular society, horizons of revolt that are immanent to every networked form of life. These horizons aren't spatial, in the sense that they suggest that a zone of revolt can be found definitively outside of the reticular society, but rather are historical, in the sense that they float like infinitely thin lines between the history of networked domination and other *undetermined and uncomputed times*, lines that mark *a separation from the world of separation*, lines that can only ever be drawn at the end of the reticular society. These horizons orient and attract lines of flight toward them—the flight from *the recognizable to the incipherable*, the flight from *the interoperable to the inoperable*, and the flight from *reticulation to abolition*—each of which, like memories of what has yet to arrive, imagine new constellations of relations and forms that bring ruin to all of the networked symmetries that circulate life as a means of circulating death.

153.

In the flight from the recognizable to the incipherable, lives invent, experiment with, and cultivate methods of evading and extracting themselves from the informatic capture that tirelessly heaves its nets across all of society. The incipherable works against two dimensions of this capture, allowing lives to elude being enciphered—being represented, coded, and written as data—as well as to escape being deciphered—being recognized, decoded, and read as data. If the networked enciphering and deciphering of life as digital information facilitates and formally sustains the present order, its circulatory and informatic *archē*, then the incipherable arises simply *as pure anarchy*, as the unrepresentable and unrecognizable *disordering of life and lived experience*.

154.

In contrast to the digital domination of the reticular society, the incipherable has no need of validation, identification, or confirmation. Incipherability doesn't exist in a binary state of true or false, in which something is either totally exposed and recorded or vanishingly imperceptible and opaque, but rather is lived in *degrees and intensities*, like a crowd that energetically comes to life or the cool that finally arrives on a summer's night. The question is thus not whether a life is or isn't incipherable, but in *what capacities and dimensions lives manage to live incipherably*.

155.

Incipherable life can be cultivated in a plurality of everyday experiences just as it might be in the incendiary turmoil of revolts, during free community lunches, hikes through forests, prisoner-letter-writing nights, and reading groups organized by friends just as during pipeline blockades, anti-fascist marches, migrant caravans, feminist strikes, and the building of encampments in the hearts of metropolises. A life can be totally documented and surveilled at school or work yet nonetheless develop other parts of their life that elude such recognition and representation, slowly cultivating and accruing an incipherability that provides a means of inconspicuous escape and unanticipated attacks. It is perhaps when a life appears to offer themself up most completely as an exposed surface that they can most effortlessly pass through an apparatus undetected, just as it is when a life appears to most convincingly play their predicted and assigned part that their revolt can arise as the most unruly and dangerous form of surprise.

156.

In lives and relations between lives, the incipherable takes form as that which casts collective shadows that thwart informatic capture, as that which increases many lives' potential to abscond from society's subsumptive apprehension, and as that which finds ways of communicatively relaying concepts, tactics, desires, knowledges, solidarities, memories, and imaginations between lives that aren't immediately enveloped and folded back into the circulating domination that aspires to encipher and decipher each and every dimension of life and lived activity. The incipherable should not be confused with escapist fantasies of living off the grid, insular conspiracies held privately by exclusive radical cliques, or the gilded blockchains where software engineers conspire to anonymously accumulate their wealth. Rather, the incipherable finds life in those practices that nurture, proliferate, and intensify *the shared potential of living with one another incipherably*. In the quiet of the shade, lives can be totally present with one another and yet remain fugitively unexposed.

157.

There is something ineradicably incipherable in each and every life, a personal refuge that can never be informatically captured, and sheltering and safeguarding this singular form of the incipherable is often what allows individual lives to survive and persevere through the immiseration of networked society. However, so long as the incipherable remains tethered and curtailed to isolated lives alone, it expresses absolutely no threat to the informatic order that digitally subsumes all of society. *The intimate and private knowledge that one's own life has not been wholly reduced to the society that dominates it* must serve instead, like chains of islands erupting across seas of solitude, as the very ground on which lives can build the capacity to reach out to other lives that also are not entirely dominated, that may have developed distinct means of escaping domination, and that might possibly offer ways of *thickening and cultivating those parts of one another that remain autonomous, creative, and free.*

158.

The incipherable thrives in noncoded, dim, and blurry forms of intimacy that constitute asocial and unrecognizable ways of living with others, that open lines of communication that are not plugged back into the totality from which they emerge, that allow for what is incipherable in each life to bridge out into collective forms of incipherability. The incipherable here emerges as a means of revolt precisely when it is assembled in those fragile, unfixed, and mobile sets of relations where something comes to *be shared and spreads but is not subsumed*, where something comes to *circulate and be held in common but is not captured.*

159.

If compelled to define and describe life in a way that is distinct from the enciphered and deciphered lives of the reticular society, one place to begin would be with all of the forms of living that resist death. One of the ways this lived resistance to death takes shape is as an escape from recognition and representation, and thus from the forms of subsumption and subjugation that are informatically imposed on life as individuated and isolated identities. The more densely a life comes to be recognized and represented as a particularly identified form of life—as a profession, an amount of debt, a familial role, a nationality, a set of credentials, a criminal history, a medical file, a party member—the more defined, constrained, fixed, and restricted the ways that life lives can come to be. So much of culture is concerned with indefinitely simulating youth, not because there is something about growing older that is inherently unfree but rather because lives have a social tendency to accumulate more and more recognized and represented identities as they age and thus come to be increasingly crowded and constrained by the coded forms of life they're compelled to live within. To remain autonomous is to live in opposition to set functions and fixed roles, to be free to creatively live in ways that remain unbound by codes, to live life as an endless experimentation with what living can possibly mean and become.

160.

The reticular society's recognition and representation of life as data allows it to impose functions on lives, aspiring to dynamically *encipher programmed destinies onto life's autonomy*. Each new informatic representation assigned to life helps to further determine and thus deaden it, algorithmically collapsing life into ever more identified lives that become increasingly indistinguishable from the interoperable machines that govern them. The incipherable proceeds as a form of revolt that opposes all recognition and representation in defense of what lives, as a form of revolt that Catherine Malabou speaks of as a life-and-death struggle against death, as a form of revolt that breaks away from any fixed, imposed, or coded relationship to identity in favor of what remains unidentifiably free. In the struggle to cultivate new ways of living, lives will have to be willing to let many identities die and decompose along the way.

161.

In the key of incipherable revolt, there is no such thing as a recognized or represented class of life that is itself opposed to networked domination, only lives that struggle against being dominated as a consequence of society's recognition and representation. The proliferation of uprisings at the beginning of the twenty-first century that proceeded without the need for a recognizable subject of history nor a desire to be represented politically should be understood as collective expressions of the incipherable, as the circulating insurgent desire to live as a growing turbulence within the enciphering and deciphering operations of network domination. Just as Édouard Glissant conjured a right to opacity, here too we can echo and extend a call for incipherable forms of life that can struggle and be in solidarity with one another *without any need to fix, identify, recognize, or become the same as one another*, refusing the integrated separation of binary selves and others by embracing *the multiplicity of life that is irreducible to any possible partition or unification.*

162.

The incipherable necessarily eschews dialectical negation in favor of a multiplication of elisions, not seeking to confront technologies of recognition and representation with new forms but rather to never be detected by the sensor or appear on the screen at all. Here the incipherable emerges not as an addition to nor as a subtraction from a network totality, but rather as a form of existence that is entirely incommensurable with the arithmetical calculations and computations of network domination. If informatic capture functions to identify and individuate life so that life's relations can be recursively reconstituted on the basis of recognized and represented identities, if its function is to digitally separate life and then communicatively integrate and subsume it on that basis, then the incipherable is what remains fundamentally *intangible and unintelligible* to the society that incessantly reaches out to grasp everything as data.

163.

While the incipherable remains formally asymmetric to recognition and representation, it nonetheless can still be fleetingly glimpsed in data that has been corrupted, in fingerprints that have been smudged, in words whispered beneath the turbulent passage of the wind, in scarves wrapped around faces at demonstrations, in unmapped friendships maintained across continents, in clandestine meetings held in squatted gardens, and in every aspect of life that manages to defer or defy being registered or recorded by society's immense capture. Beyond the reticular society's insatiable hunger for data, there are ensembles of lives that insist on living in ways that elude being devoured and consumed as such.

164.

Incipherable offensives against the reticular society must ultimately come to be devastating, not only dismantling this installation of power or dispersing that concentration of domination but eventually coming to *make the world itself radically unrecognizable*. An incipherable attack might appear as the irreversible encryption of debt records, biometric databases, or criminal files that effectively erases them from the registers of domination, seizing the criminal means of ransomware as an insurgent means of revolt. It could equally emerge as a game organized between friends who compete in teams to see who can disable the most surveillance devices across a city in a week, making a playful performance of the destruction of panoptic urban technologies. The incipherable thus blossoms in what Alexander R. Galloway and Eugene Thacker theorized as the tactics of nonexistence, which they exemplify in the shining of a laser into a camera's optical sensor, which disables it and thus allows lives to appear and yet not be recognized or represented at all by society's immense informatic capture. Because enciphering and deciphering are fundamentally relational processes, the incipherable can thus arise offensively as the destruction of whatever technologies sustain the relations between lives and data just as it can emerge autonomously as the cultivation of relations that are not subsumed by the technologies that aspire to capture and circulate all of life as codes.

165.

The incipherable necessarily precludes positive solidarity, or the forms of solidarity that are premised on the recognition of this or that identity, and instead engages in forms of negative solidarity that *have no need to identify or recognize other lives* in order to be able to join in struggle with them. The first dimension of this negative solidarity takes shape in a common struggle against what collectively dominates life, aiming to disable and dismantle the technologies of representation and recognition that function to informatically capture and digitally partition lives apart. The second dimension of incipherability's negative solidarity unfolds as providing for life's needs, developing and expanding access to diverse forms of sustenance and care whose access isn't dependent on being verified or cataloged as this or that identity, whose forms of interdependency always have the effect of decreasing life's dependency on networked society. Revolt can thus organize itself around this axiom: *Each diminishment of domination further empowers lives to care for and sustain one another, just as each magnification of lives' capacity to care further empowers life to confront domination.* These complementary dimensions of negative solidarity are nothing less than *forms of love without need of identity*, forms of affinity and intimacy and militancy that *abandon any need to determine or decide what a life is* in favor of learning *what lives desire from one another and what lives desire to become.*

166.

The incipherable should be understood as an essential part of the autonomy that runs through every horizon of liberatory struggle, an autonomy that is lived both fugitively and creatively. Autonomy entails escaping from the oppressive forms that are imposed on life as well as dismantling whatever dominates life by imposing forms on it, but this is only worthwhile if it is also simultaneously part of a movement that empowers life to engage in the autonomous *expression and cultivation of its own form*. To become autonomous is both to become free of the domination that compels life to live trapped within this or that coded form of life and to become free to *live many different lives over the course of a life*. Autonomy here extends across the space that exists between the destitution of power and the empowering of life, two insurgent dimensions of revolt that need not be separated in theory or practice.

167.

In a society so densely structured by calculation and computation, there is no quantitative accumulation of revolt that can ultimately undo the totality that it rises up against. No amount of isolated acts, no matter how numerous, can overcome or exceed the society that hungers to analyze, digitize, track, circulate, and model each fleeting fluctuation away from its rule. The capitalist order of the world cannot be defeated in parts, subtracted piece by piece, but must have its form negated as a whole. In the largest demonstrations that have been organized in the twenty-first century, various authorities have been happy to release the numbers of those who participated, making clear that they are documenting those in the streets and that they embrace forms of dissent they can count and tally as just another variable. Against this recuperative calculation, the incipherable must instead be driven toward a fundamentally qualitative transformation of life, toward the cultivation and intensification of ways of living and forms of struggle that cannot be enumerated by the social order but rather, like lightning storms that create electric bridges between earth and sky, become attractors that *more and more intensely draw lives together into a struggle to totally destroy what now so totally organizes and dominates life.*

168.

The flight from the interoperable to the inoperable takes shape as that which no longer works, as that which is useless, as that which is even less than a refusal because even refusing remains at least partially accounted for within the programs of domination as errors or glitches or exceptions to be corrected by future optimizations and updates. The inoperable explodes the present order by short-circuiting it and causing its programs to halt, terminating the productive and subsumptive motion of society by blowing out its fuses. If the operable is what works and the interoperable is what works together, the inoperable is play and rest but also sabotage and strikes, arising as what stops things from working or as what never worked at all.

169.

The inoperable is the summer blackout that invites everyone to meet with one another on the street and relax, the traffic jam that creates an opportunity to step out of a car and kick a ball around on a freeway, a social media outage that prompts lives to put their screens away, an occupied lecture hall that cancels classes and creates time to talk and reflect, or a computer virus that encrypts corporate databases and gives everyone a day off of their jobs. In a society in which everything is compelled to function together seamlessly online, in which all of culture and politics and the economy and thus society emerge as a unified productive force that interoperably advances and circulates the devastation of the reticular society, inoperability invites life to *relinquish all of the ways it has been compelled to be useful and incapacitate all of the ways it is used*.

170.

The reticular society's compulsory interoperability, its demand that everything work together *or else*, is sustained and defended in part by a form of extortion that is articulated across two scales. On the scale of the individual, if a life doesn't work as they are expected and compelled to, if they don't submit to the social destiny axiomatically and algorithmically generated for them by networks, then the reticular society effectively abandons that life, cutting them off from what life needs and holding them up as a warning of what happens when a life fails to perform as they should. On the scale of society, if everything doesn't continue to work together as it presently does, if the economy doesn't continue to expand and politics don't continue to bear down on and police everything, then the reticular society warns that all of society and everything it provides will rapidly collapse, depriving not just a life but all life of what it needs to sustain itself, as supermarkets and malls go barren, networks and other infrastructures go dark, and law and order evaporate into thin air. Even the smallest of interruptions of society's smooth operation—a bank closing, user numbers shrinking, trade slowing—are presented as existential threats to civilization that call for the most dramatic interventions and remedies. This extortion is perhaps most simply formulated and intuitively understood as the choice that life is persistently compelled to make *between work and the abyss*.

171.

The reticular society always proceeds as an endless series of destructive contingencies that only serve to recursively produce the necessity of the reticular society, in which the catastrophes produced by work produce the need to work more. There is no real opposition to destruction or violence, only an opposition to whatever slows the operations of networked domination and progress. The reticular society is thus able to condemn the vandalism of a riot as excessive but excuse the violence of a border as necessary, to condemn a port blockade as hurting the economy but excuse the criminalization of strikes as part of a need to attract investment, to condemn eco-saboteurs who impede the construction of a police training facility in a forest as terrorists but excuse mass extinctions and the devastation of ecosystems as an inevitable externality of society's development, to condemn a group who takes groceries from a corporate supermarket and distributes them freely to their neighbors as criminals but excuse the mass circulation of wealth across networks of offshore tax havens as a healthy expression of global markets. All of the destruction that follows from society's normal operation is retroactively and recursively used to justify the need for society itself. The speed of networked progress that obliterates more and more of what's in its path only produces a heightened sense that society must continue to accelerate in hopes of overcoming the rubble and averting a fatal crash. The arrival of capitalism simultaneously gave birth to two futures: one in which *life is eventually able to bring an end to capitalism* and another in which *capitalism eventually brings an end to life*.

172.

The reticular society's extortion that declares that lives must continue to interoperably work together or society itself may fall apart is ultimately only a mask that works to cover over the desolation left in the trail of all work. This desolation is experienced existentially by each life as an arrest of its potential within the delimited and programmed possibilities of society, in which forms of use that are algorithmically identified as productive and profitable come to preclude every other potential use, in which the singularity of life's creativity is captured and recuperated as an isolated and discrete component of society's machines. At larger scales, the desolation produced by work has been historically expressed as the digitized execution of war and genocide, as the persistent surveillance and mass detention of undesirables, as the accumulation of migrant camps at the edge of border checkpoints and worker slums at the edge of smart cities, as climate catastrophes and mass extinctions, and as ever more fragile health care, food, and water systems. While there is no shortage of acolytes of the reticular society that will plead that it is absolutely necessary to keep the global machine running or else all is lost, that things may be bad but that anything else would be far worse, that we just have to introduce new incentives or implement new regulations, they cannot hide from the truth that there is *no form of insurrectionary violence that can rival the violence of the present society when it is working well, optimally and interoperably, as it is intended and designed to*. Inoperativity is not only a refusal of work but a refusal of work's expanding and intensifying desolation, which encroaches on each life and on all life generally. *That things continue to work well is the catastrophe.*

173.

All property under capitalism is structured at its foundation by the right to exclusive use, in which the owner of this factory or that online resource possesses the power to dictate the terms and conditions under which it can be utilized. This private dimension of property is then linked to capitalist markets, which add an inclusive dimension to property's exclusivity, providing anyone with enough capital access to what otherwise is guarded and withheld. In the reticular society, all forms of property relations undergo a further transformation that introduces a communicative dimension to the exclusivity of property, exposing capital, commodities, computers, and lives to the networked domination of use, transforming all property into minimally discrete components while making them maximally available to network commands and controls that interoperably suffuse everything. In one direction everything becomes more privatized, exclusive, and closed off and in the other more connected, accessible, and open, and as a result the ever more numerous and diverse means of production and control accumulate an *exclusive capacity to act on and utilize what has been brought inclusively within reach.* Data centers and digitized homes, factories and farms, software and subjects are all connected as *separated resources that can then be put to use by separated forces.* Every rise in social communicability is thus mirrored in the rise of a corresponding social utility, parsing life ever more finely to include it ever more totally in the interoperable exchange, coordination, and domination of all of life's activities.

174.

The interoperability of the reticular society moves to integrate all of life's means seamlessly together in order to redirect them toward the reticular society's singular ends, communicatively grasping each life as a means of furthering the networked subsumption and subordination of all life. Interoperability is concerned with maximizing the work that life can perform in cooperation with the networked systems that also function to minimize the resistance that life can enact against them, compelling lives to become increasingly optimized and useful as they become increasingly servile and subdued. The flight from the interoperable to the inoperable thus involves a life *depriving themself of all usefulness*, and in so doing *liberating life's means from the networked domination of society's ends*.

175.

Against society's interoperability, the inoperable arises in forms of use that do not contract into the discrete enclaves of this or that form of property, nor do they open themselves up to be used and made to work by whatever commands the most power in society. The inoperable thrives in all of the lived activities that are not fixed, tethered, or chained to the managers, algorithms, markets, and networks that aim to optimize and organize all activity, in all of the lived activities that are not subordinated to nor subsumed within reticulated ends, in all of the lived activities that arise as pure means. One of the central functions of the networked privation, dispossession, and monopolization of all use is to compel lives to forget all of the things *life remains capable of doing*, and thus the inoperative can be understood simply as the *lived reclamation of every potential at life's disposal* that cuts off the reticular society's access to the same.

176.

Détournement is one of the practices that can cultivate the inoperable by stealing what has been put to use by society and militantly experimenting with new forms of use. By recuperating what society has recuperated, dispossessing society of what it has dispossessed life of, and undoing the exclusive inclusion that runs through the interoperability of the reticular society, détournement emerges as a form of creative and autonomous use unconcerned with and unconstrained by property. The forms of détournement that were deployed by the Situationists in the twentieth century focused on the spectacular dimensions of use that dominated the social forms of their time, remaking and reassembling the posters, films, photographs, comic strips, and magazines that visually mediated and symbolically colonized lived reality. In the reticular society, détournement must necessarily go further and expansively widen its formal reach, playfully appropriating and hijacking anything that has been subsumed online. Everything that networks aspire to grasp as tools, lives must struggle to reclaim as weapons.

177.

As everything has come to be symbolically integrated into the informatic and communicative order of the reticular society as data on networks—grocery stores, roads, office buildings, ports, schools, police vans, factories, museums, server farms, banks, and distribution warehouses are all abstracted and subsumed alike online—everything thus has the potential to be détourned. Détournement thus can and should still be formalized as subway ads that have been repurposed to extol the virtues of the riot or as recut police films that are subverted to narratively depict the irreversible collapse of law and order, but it also now can and should additionally be expressed in the rerouting and hijacking of the broader world that has been so densely colonized by informatic division and online circulation. A bus used to carry tech workers to suburban campuses can be stopped and transformed into part of a barricade to make room for a neighborhood festival, police fences can be dismantled and reassembled into public sculptures, and a vinyl advertisement can be torn down from a billboard and hung between two street poles to be used as an outdoor cinema screen at a protest encampment. A networked camera surveying a détourned world should persistently scan for recognizable objects and trackable activities and only spit out ever greater sums of random strings and empty arrays.

178.

Détournement arises like art and poetry that render their respective forms inoperative and, in so doing, remind us of the breadth of their formal potential. A sentence becomes not an order or instruction but an image or a flood of emotion, just as a piece of metal becomes not an architectural feature or computer component but a cloud or a sleeping cat. When deprived of their coded use, things in the world have the capacity to open us to the potential of what is noncoded, arising against this world as otherworldly forces that can be as dangerous as they are beautiful. This form of détournement is perhaps practiced most virtuosically by children, who so effortlessly refuse the world's order and invent new uses, encountering a plastic toy gun in the playground and then waving it around in the air as a soaring bird, or picking up a history book as a musical instrument that can be played by ripping each of its pages out in different directions and at varying speeds. Détournement invites the discovery of new potential uses that are discordant with the world as it is presently tuned, clashing violently as *a form of disorganization against the social organization of the useful*, and thus appears as a weapon against the totalitarian interoperability that aspires to be the sole programmer of life's potential. The things and lives that have been put to use by the reticular society should be taken up and reinvented as *the creative artillery to blast the present society's order apart*.

179.

The incipherable and the inoperable effectively converge in forms of détournement that sweep across everything that networks take as their objects, robbing things of their socially recognized uses and poietically inventing new uses in them. A tear gas canister becomes a flower pot, a military outpost is transformed into a bird sanctuary, a computer is reformatted and becomes a pirate digital library, a fast food restaurant becomes a community kitchen, a monument is torn down and becomes part of a building occupation's barricade, a private art gallery is remade into a free clinic, and a concrete separation wall has holes punched through it and becomes a canvas for collective murals and messages passed back and forth between lovers. Everywhere things can be creatively and militantly reappropriated and resurrected in forms that are of no use to domination.

180.

In the flight from the interoperable to the inoperable, revolt against the reticular society emerges not as a revolt against technology in itself but rather as a revolt against *the way technology has been socially organized and strategically deployed*. There are many technologies that are presently integrated into the reticular society that life may find new uses for after the reticular society has been abolished, just as there are others that will have to be dismantled, recycled, incinerated, or forgotten. The inoperable thus has a relation to technology determined by life's autonomy, and thus necessarily emerges against the informatic capture, networked organization, and total integration of technology into the domination of life. The tech industry megaconferences that annually lay claim to the limitless capacity of new technologies to further unleash economic, cultural, and political powers only make clear the extreme poverty and captivity of their imaginations, in which even things they describe as revolutionary and totally disruptive can only be imagined as minor extensions of the way the world has already been organized and put to use. Like an ATM that has been hacked to replace its menus with lines of insurrectionary poetry, détournement is a threat that is articulated in all of the potential ways society's technologies can be stolen and smuggled away, hacked and reprogrammed, dismantled and reassembled, terminated and then resuscitated on life's autonomous terms.

181.

The inoperable arises perhaps most clearly today in the manifestly destituent character of the numerous uprisings that have erupted across the planet in the first decades of the twenty-first century, uprisings that have often been formalized as movements without demands. A movement without demands is a movement that cannot be appeased or placated, cannot be negotiated with or nudged in this or that direction, cannot be communicated with or reconnected, cannot be so easily incorporated back into the networked orchestration and oversight of use. A movement without demands is a movement that cannot be used by political parties to advance their agendas, cannot be used to repress the more unruly parts of itself, and cannot be used to reform this or that system. A movement without demands remains inoperable precisely because its use remains determined only by those who cultivate, sustain, and give form to it.

182.

Movements without demands emerged out of the ruins of movements that were born in search of recognition. Like noisy constituents who act out only to attract the attention of their elected officials, or deluded prisoners who seek reprieve by attempting to befriend their guards, movements drawn to be recognized in this or that form are typically accommodated and recognized just as they wish, and thus come to sit like carefully framed photographs that only collect dust and have no consequence at all. A movement without demands is thus best understood as a form of collective revolt that has no attachment to what domination desires to identify, recognize, or pick up as technologies or tools, aiming to be of no use in the hopes of finding the means of autonomously and freely remaking the world. It aspires to break away from the interoperability maintained between life and networks that keeps everything communicating and functioning, to snap out of the dependence on the very forms that integrate and isolate life, and to incipherably break apart the fixed identities that trap life in the ways it has been recognized as useful by bosses, by politicians, by police, by algorithms, and by the totality of networked society.

183.

In some of the most incendiary revolts of the twenty-first century, which managed to pry open disordered fissures in the order of the world, the questions posed by insurrectionary forces came to be answered not by those on the streets but by police commanders and military leadership who decided to side with or against the erupting struggle. Whether choosing to fire on the crowds or detain this or that head of state, the power of the military and the police to decide, *the decision itself*, effectively closed avenues to the further expansion and intensification of revolt. Revolts must aspire to pose questions for which no answer is socially available, opening questions in such an inoperative and incipherable fashion that they cannot be closed within society's present form. The form of destitution and abolition that is articulated by movements without demands arrives as what refuses to be decided on, as *an infinite loop or memory leak or fork bomb that causes the programs of a system to slow and eventually crash*, as the indecision that short-circuits domination. Like an email link that downloads a virus and bricks a computer, any attempt by society to subsume or suppress a revolt should only further suspend its operations. Revolt ultimately is not a matter of seizing the means of domination nor of fleetingly transgressing its rule, but simply of *rendering domination itself increasingly inexecutable*.

184.

The domination of life in the reticular society can be measured in the accumulation of society's connected separation, in which each new division and partition serves as a new means of subsumption and desolation. Every calculated advance of networked society is thus formally bound to the informatic partition and circulatory integration of lived reality, possibilizing further exploitation, alienation, and dispossession just as it possibilizes novel forms of accumulation, repression, and extraction. In the *flight from reticulation to abolition*, we can thus locate the most extensive and intensive form of revolt, a form of attack oriented against the connected separation of networks that is the most elementary form of the reticular society and thus a form of attack that *can express itself potentially anywhere and everywhere within it*.

185.

The flight from reticulation to abolition is invested in a lived autonomy that cannot arise from measures that solely aim to reform or reclaim the connected separations of the network form, as it is connected separation itself that is the foundational technology through which the violence of domination has been and continues to be realized socially and historically. Abolitionist gestures, those that aim to *dismantle and destroy the social logic of reticulation as such*, search for paths toward autonomy that defy being rerouted and reprogrammed within the cycles of informatic separation and circulating integration that flow all around. Abolition arises as whatever renders life less compatible with, less dependent on, less captured within, and less determined by the networked world of connected separation that lays waste to life.

186.

One of the ways abolition is realized is in the refusal of friend and enemy distinctions as they have been coded as identities in the reticular society. The degree to which struggles and revolts unfold on the basis of the ways in which society has already been separated and connected is also the degree to which those struggles and revolts are effectively limited and constrained in advance, curtailing them to the forms and formations, classifications and classes, that are themselves part of what must be undone through struggle. Rather than fight to identify and parse between friends and enemies, it is rather revolts themselves that can reveal which lives cultivate and further advance abolition and which lives only advance its recuperation, restraint, or repression. We can simply find joy in *everything and everyone that renders ourselves and our struggles more powerful*, that *increases our shared capacity to think, act, create, imagine, and resist*. Love and hate must be detached and torn away from this or that enciphered class of life, from this or that social identity, and found again in the very relations that must be strengthened and cultivated or weakened and abandoned in the process of struggle itself.

187.

In revolts against networked domination, lives inevitably find themselves drawn toward two dead ends sustained by the reticular society. One terminus is formalized as a pure assault on the forms of domination that suffuse lived reality, as an act of wholly throwing oneself against the machines that subordinate life to a suicidal degree. In lives that see themselves already as martyrs, escape is found not by bringing an end to domination but rather by striking a final autonomous blow that brings an end to what was dominated, that brings an end to themselves. This register *maximizes the force of living*, but ultimately *at the cost of life itself*. The second terminus is found on the other end of the line, in which a steady retreat from domination into forms of relative stability and comfort work to preserve life by tactically avoiding and mitigating the excesses of domination. Exhausted lives come to struggle not against domination but rather for little interludes of relative stability and calm within it. Here *life is held tightly and close*, but *at the cost of living*. Both of these dead ends represent binary outputs of what has already been accounted for in the reticular society, each of which neutralizes life in formally incongruent ways but whose strategic outcome is nonetheless precisely the same.

188.

Abolition necessarily resists suicidal attacks or perpetual retreats, opting instead to opportunistically escape and tactically dismantle networked domination wherever it is found. Abolition thus *refuses the clean binary separation* between those who revolt and those who do not, between total insurrection and defeated passivity, instead *seeking in every relation and every encounter a means of undoing domination and ultimately moving to expand those relations at a rate and scale that exceeds the subsumptive capacity of the reticular society*. If resistance and revolt are never cleanly external to power, this is only all the more helpful, as it means they are already present in every particle of society and thus it only becomes a question of multiplying and intensifying what already saturates all of lived reality. In every moment, life, and relation, *new weapons lay to be seized*. Abolition cannot be contained to this or that radical activist milieu, elite intellectual circle, or exclusive subcultural scene but rather emerges across all of those forms of life that contain the potential to erupt against the reticular society, to erupt as the incipherable and inoperable lives that escape, circulate, and spread precisely because of the way they formally set themselves apart from life's connected separation.

189.

Even in those cases where friend and enemy distinctions appear to most consistently and clearly express themselves as coded identities—in confrontations with security forces, with the police, with soldiers—struggles must refuse to constitute themselves exclusively on those oppositional and binary terms. Abolition instead necessarily emerges asymmetrically in relation to what it desires to abolish, *refusing all formal correspondence, resemblance, and equivalence with what it is drawn to extinguish and bury in this world.* This asymmetry can emerge tactically and conceptually, creatively and relationally, always seeking to *intensify the dissimilarity between the order of the world and the disorders that erupt within it*. Whenever society aims to expand itself in new regimes of work and advance its smooth functioning, asymmetric revolts must *proliferate pockets of friction and resistance*. Whenever networks seek to subsume all of space and time as a totality, asymmetric revolts must *counter with a frothing multiplicity of insurgent heres and nows* that fight from the precise specificities of wherever and whenever they are. Whenever various forces of domination aspire to impose or reestablish forms of order, asymmetric revolts must respond with *a kaleidoscopic explosion of new disorders*. Lives must ultimately struggle to break the networked mirror that imposes its reticulated symmetry everywhere and find many new forms of life in the asymmetric multiplicity that shines across its shattered debris.

190.

The asymmetry of revolt can be seen at work in demonstrations that have learned that their endurance depends not on beating the police at their own game, but on *inventing and playing games of their own*. Riot police desire to get close to lives, to compress and kettle them into tight spaces where they can be better surrounded and surveilled, to grasp and grab hold of them, to manipulate them and bruise them and violate them and concuss them and break them, and ultimately to detain, totally document, criminally charge, and densely encipher the violence of society on them. Cops literally remake and reformalize their own bodies to these ends, lifting weights, downing steroids, and training in bulky armor. Militant street demonstrations that have managed to claim victories against the police thus have worked asymmetrically by experimenting with and practicing an *art of distances*, building barricades to hold off baton charges, raining down rocks and other objects to push away lines of cops, using forms of communication that elude surveillance, and moving things into the streets and setting them on fire to slow down water cannons and trucks filled with snatch squads. Forces of domination aspire to capture all conflict within the logic of a binary confrontation—lines of police breaking and brutalizing lines of protestors—while revolts benefit instead by propagating and protracting confrontations to such a degree that each line of confrontation becomes lost in an expanding commotion, noise, and turbulence. Asymmetry here doesn't take shape in the avoidance or embrace of any particular conflict, but in *the diverse intensification and formal multiplication of new antagonisms and revolts*.

191.

Asymmetric revolts remain incommensurable and incongruent with what they desire to destroy, and thus live as a formal threat to what dominates life. When the police do manage to capture a life that had been loudly chanting slogans and carrying a banner in the street, in the back of the van and in the interrogation room and in court that same life finds no need to express anything and finds *the purest of joys in the asymmetry of their silence*. When the police charge forward and aspire to strike a final blow, demonstrations win by dispersing and later reassembling on terrains and terms of their own choosing, never ceding the strategic form to what desires to capture and extinguish them. As police attempt to kettle and block and surround, revolts can dynamically split and redistribute themselves so that police find themselves overwhelmed by a constellation of disorders that flicker in and out of existence like fireflies in the night. On police radios you can hear the fear in captains' voices as they realize that the one march they hoped to repress has splintered into a hundred roving groups spreading out across and reclaiming a city. Asymmetry is sand against gears, salt water against circuits, acid against card readers, smoke against spotlights, mud against tires, jamming devices against drones, paint against windshields, logic bombs against code, thought against recognition, poetry against information, commonality against privation, creativity against domination, life against death.

192.

The question of abolition ultimately emerges not as a question of constituting a force strong enough to defeat society's repressive forces in some kind of final confrontation, nor in appealing to those forces to side with and defend those in struggle. Any strategic or tactical victory against soldiers, police, or security forces in the streets can only ever be fleeting, and any kind of prolonged military struggle only reproduces the binary structure of society and thus can only end in defeat. Abolition rather must pursue the path of *corroding and destituting the very social forms that allow for such forces to exist and persist at all*, building fault lines through their informatic foundations, propagating like a parasitic fungus through their rhizomatic infrastructures, creeping like corrosive rust through their interoperable components. This particular avenue of revolt aims to move from the *competition between forms* to the *cancellation of forms*, to a revolt whose intensity has reached such a degree that the social forms that constitute domination *can no longer reproduce themselves nor endure*.

193.

Scrawled across walls in Cairo, Mexico City, Hong Kong, Oakland, Santiago, Hamburg, Jakarta, Montreal, Abuja, Haifa, Madrid, Atlanta, Athens, and Istanbul, the four letters *ACAB* are an articulation of the hatred not simply of those who dominate but more fundamentally to *the hatred of domination's form* that has been historically copied and pasted across every possible social context, just as when French rioters chant "*tout le monde déteste la police*," they can so confidently do so only because of the weaponized detachments, caustic indifferences, and vacated lives that so universally compose the ranks of police forces across the world. It is only when revolts manage to cut a form off from what sustains it, when the flows and structures and programs that support a form collapse, when a form only functions to dampen rather than magnify power, that its actuality tends to fade away like the snow in spring. The only thing that might rival the beauty of streets that have been reclaimed from and cleared of the police is perhaps the moment when *police no longer can imagine remaining who they are*, when *they abandon their precincts to looters and open the cells of the prisons they guarded*, when *they out of fear or desperation or loathing find themselves chasing a way out*, when *they pile up their uniforms and set them aflame in hopes of turning their very form of life to ash*.

194.

In conjunction with the forms of asymmetry that are cultivated in militant practices of revolt, theorizing also emerges as an asymmetric practice for abolition. Even as theorizing is situated within the connected separation that suffuses all life, forms of thought can nonetheless cultivate asymmetries when intellectual relations and exchanges between lives manage to resonate transversally *across the fragmented terrain they find themselves in*. Among the primary tasks of theory is to break out of the discrete and fixed positions it is so often tied down to and defused within, exploding beyond university enclaves and activist milieus so that it can *traverse and translate itself across many diverse lives, languages, situations, and struggles*, anarchically moving across and against the symmetrical order of the world. Just as collective practices allow us to take joy in the power of acting with others, theory allows us to *take joy in the power of thinking with others*, of theorizing in modes that are only available when they are enacted by and between many lives. Theorizing the world collectively involves contemplating the particularity of one's own life as well as other lives, but to do so from a position that emerges between lives and thus from a position that is irreducible to any particular life. Theorizing with others is incompatible with life's connected separation, arising instead as an encounter between the distinct potentials of diverse lives that produces an intellectual power held in common by them.

195.

One of the ways the reticular society inflicts itself most forcefully and violently on the minds of the living is in the binary divide it carves between the possible and the impossible, digitally separating and cleaving reality into managed sets of what appears reasonable and what eludes even the imagination. The possibilities to be this or that networked form of life, to take on this or that job, to go into this or that amount of debt, to be distracted by this or that piece of content, and to compromise in this or that way are all algorithmically churned out and circulated everywhere, all of which ultimately sustain the appearance of the reticular society as the only possible outcome of a history that is built on the impossibility of living any other way. Against the clean and sharp cut between possible and impossible worlds and lives, theory struggles to make *what is presently impossible intelligible*, and in so doing aims to help cultivate and proliferate its potentiality. It is precisely the potential of life that overcomes the digital split between the possible and impossible, a potential that is expressed in forms of theory and revolt that aim to shatter the imposed symmetry between what can and cannot exist. Against a totalitarian digitality there is a theorization of a multiplicity that exists not on the binary terms of *what is* and *what is not* but on the terrain of *what has the potential to be*. What is asymmetric in theory arises precisely from this unbalance between the possible and the potential, between *the powers imposed on and the powers cultivated by life*.

196.

The asymmetries expressed in theories and practices can be further developed and elaborated by multiplying and refracting them through one another, never letting theory or practice imprint itself on the other but rather allowing their potentials to mutually transform one another in ways that intensify the unruly disorder of revolts. Nothing is accomplished by assigning primacy to ideas or gestures, but there is much to be gained by proliferating the volatile exchanges that can take place between them. *There has never been a revolt that did not also draw its participants to conceptualize and theorize their situation in new ways*, just as *there has never been a concept or theory that hasn't needed to search for opportunities to be tested and revised when conflicts ignite and unfold.* Across tactical inheritances and intellectual traditions, the relationships between theory and practice flourish most profusely when they refuse to be neatly distinguished or separated, never allowing themselves to be captured by isolated specialists or celebrity experts and instead flowering across as many locations and lives as possible, arising as the dynamic multiplication of *intellectual militancies* and *militant intellects*. What is theorized and what is put into practice thrives in their manifold layering and shedding, allowing for wild assemblages of concepts and tactics to be activated and abandoned as needed, always aiming to throw the order of domination ever further off balance with *a relentlessly creative proliferation of novel asymmetries and insurgent forms*.

197.

Abolition is advanced as an asymmetric revolt that doesn't simply arrive at a relatively weakened or tamed domination of life, nor is it a form of revolt whose destination is simply its own eventual dissipation. Abolition rather demands that we disinvest from and dismantle what dominates life, but only as a means of making possible the forms of life that have been programmatically rendered impossible, of cultivating and empowering a multiplicity of socialities that will blossom in the soil of the reticular society they have managed to bury. Abolition moves to cultivate relations that make platforms increasingly unneeded and undesirable, that let platforms' valuations plummet and their user bases empty out, that empower lives and *leave the channels of networked domination increasingly deserted, powerless, and obsolete.*

198.

Abolition emerges from asymmetric forms of coexistence and interdependence that deepen their roots and expand but are not subsuming nor totalizing, that provide for what lives need and thus remove life's need for the reticular society, that allow for expanding attacks on social domination to be accompanied by the fecund experimentation with new forms of life. A life lived asymmetrically is a life that has not been reduced to another object of network circulation, that refuses to see the world and other lives as online flows of commodities, images, and data, that remains incompatible with all forms of digitized subordination and subsumption, that has stolen back their potential from the circuits of accumulation that threaten to devour all life. Asymmetric forms of life proceed as growing imbalances and turbulences within the reticular society, as insurgent variations whose frequencies and intensities grow to the degree that they destabilize and break apart what desires to manage and rule over all of life's rhythms and forms. Abolition in each instance *dreams of the end of the world* and, in so doing, *dreams of many worlds.*

199.

All of the struggles that life engages in—the struggle for life's creative autonomy, the struggle to share life with others, the struggle to shape life's common conditions, and ultimately the struggle for a classless society—offer fragile and fleeting escapes from the networked logic that otherwise subjugates and imposes a multiplicity of hierarchies on life. These struggles sustain and empower life, and in sustaining and empowering can also come to be something that contagiously spreads joy and draws lives to them. The flight from the recognizable to the incipherable, from the interoperable to the inoperable, and ultimately from reticulation to abolition should remain focused on indefinitely intensifying, expanding, and protracting life's struggles whenever and wherever they emerge, not waiting for some impossibly ideal moment, decisive systemic crisis, or final historical conjuncture but rather *threatening to arise always and everywhere within the totality that has already colonized each moment and every place*. The connectivity and commensurability of the network form must ultimately be confronted by all of those forms of life that still draw us to struggle with one another rather than only for ourselves, by those forms of life that are not wholly defeated and find ways of continuing to ignite insurrections against what subdues and subsumes, by those forms of life that express the potential of destituting and abolishing society's connected separation and thus cultivate the autonomy and creativity of what still lives. The dawn of life appears everywhere as the dusk of networked domination, as a lived movement that eclipses the reticular society and leaves many new horizons burning behind.

AFTERWORD

What Is a Repertoire?

Within the movement of history, there is an immense clamor of gestures. Hands busily place components onto circuit boards as they flow down assembly lines, and arms extend to topple the chain-link fences that surround detention camps. A finger slides across the surface of a screen, a back arches to lower a child into bed, and a tangle of bodies sprints forward and breaks through lines of police attempting to encircle a crowd on the street. At times instructed or coerced and at others conscious and free, our lives are lived as gesture upon gesture, as forms searching for their shape in the world.

Over centuries, our understanding of the gesture has narrowed to the degree that it is now seen as including only the expressive and communicative movements of the body. The gesture is in this limited and impoverished sense understood to be simply one part of a visual language, an image of movement intended only to be interpreted and read. This narrowing of the gesture's meaning was accompanied by the historical ascendance of surveillance technologies, of representative politics, and of the spectacular economy, the historical ascendance of life understood as an image. But in the etymology of *gesture* we find a far more ample concept that involves all of the ways we *carry* ourselves in the world, all of the ways a life becomes movement as it unfolds across the dimension of time. The gesture in this broader sense concerns appearance as well as action, sensuality as well as physicality, allowing us to approach life not only as something to be perceived but also as something with force. It is on the basis of this widened understanding that we can begin to diagram how the gesture gives form to the autonomy and creativity of life, as well as how mechanisms of domination and control aspire to capture and take the gesture as their own.

Gestures are improvised and invented anew every time they are enacted, but gestures are also repetitions, calling on histories of past gestures just as they too become history. To scale a cliff for the hundredth time draws from the ninety-nine other climbs that preceded it, just as it elaborates in novel ways on them and emerges as a uniquely singular climb. In this way a gesture makes use of already existing muscles, memories, instincts, and techniques that were given form and shape by past gestures, just as it reforms and reshapes them in the very process of its enactment. In one of the final scenes of Alfonso Cuarón's *Roma*, we glimpse this simultaneous invention and repetition of the gesture: After a child is rescued from the rough waves of the sea and carried to their family ashore, everyone wraps their arms around one another as they collapse together onto the sand. This embrace resembles and is a repetition of past embraces—it has a familiar intensity, duration, appearance, and form—and yet it also arises as its own novel gesture, fundamentally different from every gesture that preceded it and as unique as the time and place it unfolds within. *Repertoire* is the concept we have at our disposal for attending to this unique yet repetitive character of gestures, for seeing in the singularity of each gesture its multiplicity.

A repertoire exists not as a point between the past and future but rather as the passage through which they connect and coincide, through which past becomes future and future becomes past. It is in this sense that a repertoire gives shape to gestures that are in the process of being enacted and actualized, but the repertoire also has a temporality that cannot be so neatly contained within a finite and discrete present. When we say that a dancer has a repertoire that they have developed and is at their disposal, we don't refer to a specific gesture or set of gestures so much as *a gestural potential* that they have trained and sharpened over time in performances and rehearsals, a reservoir of past gestures that can give shape and form to gestures in the future. Any particular dance in this sense is inseparable from this potential to dance, from the repertoire through which any gesture becomes art. As Robert Hurley makes clear, to see a dance principally as a thing and not as a potential is to fall victim to the spectacular nature of society, to grasp the world as a collection of isolated commodities, objects, and images and thus to entirely miss the unruly creativity that underlies all of existence.

Because a repertoire concerns the way the potentials of life are expressed, it also has historically come to be taken as another object to be dominated as a means of capturing, reshaping, and subordinating life's potential. On the hypersurveilled and automated floors of Amazon distribution warehouses, people are hired to work as "pickers" and are tasked with collecting products from plastic bins and then placing them into cardboard delivery boxes. That the job is named after the gesture already reveals so much: The gesture is nothing less in this instance than the lived form that is captured by the economy and then made to appear as *labor*. Each picker is instructed to stand at their station facing a computer terminal that displays an image of a product, and then a vertical tower of bins is moved by a wheeled robot so that it is beside them and within arm's reach. A projector positioned above then flashes a rectangle of white light onto the target bin, which alerts the picker of the product's location and guides their hand toward it, and once the product is grasped it must then be scanned at the terminal and packed away. Automated vision systems verify that the assigned product is in the assigned box, and then an audible beep signals that the task has been completed. The picker then presses a button, is assigned another bin, which a robot delivers to their side, and the process begins again.

The Amazon warehouses and those who work within them function on the basis of a perpetual and comprehensive fragmentation, a process that first isolates a particular life as a worker and then isolates the various capacities and potentials of that life by breaking it down into ever more minute and elementary gestures. The lifting of an arm, the turn of a torso, and the movement of an eye are each taken to be isolated components of a process that can be quantified, fine-tuned, and rearranged as needed by algorithms designed to optimize each task. Once broken down and atomized as far as possible, a series of signals sent from machines then choreograph these fragmented gestures and build them up into a repertoire that is programmable and thus automatable, aspiring to reduce thought to an absolute minimum as the body of the worker becomes ever more synchronized with the system's calibrated prompts and instructions. The repertoire in this context thus doesn't reside within a life or between several lives but rather exists as code, data, and devices, subsuming and subjecting the potentials of a body to the commands and controls of networked machines. The greater the degree to which life is effectively dispossessed of its gestures and repertoires as they are captured and placed under the management of machines, the more the autonomy of life has been effectively destroyed.

Here we see the way in which the gesture is subsumed both for its physical capacity to act within and on the world—to lean, to reach, to grasp, to lift, and so on—and for its sensual existence as an image to be read by a machine and thus to be digitally captured, analyzed, and managed by networked systems. A gesture both appears and acts, and thus it can be observed and orchestrated, tracked and trained, surveilled and subsumed. Simultaneously, the very capacity to sense is taken as another component of control. Sight and hearing are no longer the means through which to experience the world so much as they are made into inputs where instructions and information can be sent. Amazon has even patented electronic bracelets that vibrate as they approach a programmed target, transforming touch itself into another feedback mechanism and further integrating life into its cybernetic loops. Life is ultimately dispossessed not only of its gestures but also its senses as they are captured and placed under the control of networked systems that aim to move bodies just as they redirect packets of data or adjust the flight path of drones.

In this most controlled of environments, everything the picker does is monitored and then modified only to be monitored and modified again in the endless cycles of networked oversight and management. Precisely how many degrees an Amazon picker must lean over to reach a bin, how quickly they must depart and return to their station during bathroom breaks, and how many microtasks they must complete every hour is thus organized online in relation to all of the other pickers laboring away nearby. Lives and their gestures are taken as discrete variables to be balanced and adjusted in relation to every other life and gesture, synthesizing the kinetic and the cybernetic so as to further subsume life, and eventually breaking bodies as the relentless acceleration and repetition of tasks erode tendons, joints, and muscles as well as any existential sense of being. This structure ultimately effectuates and sustains the *reticulation of life's gestures*, capturing them within networked systems that control the order and the form within which they are enacted. One's own gestures are reserved for some imaginary time off the clock as more and more of life is spent struggling to complete gestures that are determined by *a repertoire of the enemy*. The poetry of the gesture is slowly suffocated within this online economy of gestures, within these networked forms of social domination that impose their algorithmic order on the creative capacities of life.

The economization of the gesture was built on the foundational metaphysics of Western civilization, a system that found its first complete articulation in Aristotle's writing on ethics and politics in ancient Greece. Aristotle argued that life is composed of a series of capacities: the capacity to grow, eat, move, reproduce, and think, among others. Some of these capacities are shared in common by life across different species, but for Aristotle the capacity to reason was in essence a superior capacity and was possessed exclusively by humans, setting them apart from and ultimately above all other forms of life. The good life for Aristotle thus required rationally creating order within one's own life, but it also required rationally imposing order on those lives that lacked reason, such as animals, or had an inferior capacity to reason, such as women or slaves. A desire to impose order on oneself becomes a desire to impose order on a home, and then a city, and then a territory, and so on. The question of capacity was thus from the very beginning articulated as *a question of mastery*, a question of which capacities existed in a hierarchy above others and consequently a question of which lives should rule and which should be ruled. It is from this mastery that we must recover the gesture and the repertoire, and it is against this mastery that the struggle to break free must be waged.

The metaphysical system established by Aristotle ultimately introduces life not as something *to be lived* but rather as a set of capacities *to be used*, more or less efficiently, more or less rationally, more or less profitably. Here we see the deep intimacy of technique and technology in Western society, the way in which the art of *technê* (τέχνη) has been totally collapsed into function, operation, and instrument. The creative potentiality of life is taken as a resource to be spent and put to work, as a set of discrete actions and capacities that must be made productive, as another technology to be integrated into the machinery of the economy and the desolation it multiplies. This economization of life implicit in Aristotle's thought thus creates the conditions within which the capacities of supposedly inferior forms of life (slaves, workers, animals, children, etc.) must be mastered so their lives *do not go to waste*, so their lives *aren't misused* or *left without use*. It is here that we can see how the gesture, as a capacity, came to be exposed to the domination and rationality of the economy and thus *must at any cost be made useful*. An internal economy within each life must rationally put their own inferior capacities to their best use, but this economy then reappears as *an economy between lives* that desires to impose a rational order on life as a whole. This is nothing less than the essential diagram on which Western society was founded: a domination of one's own capacities that is bound to a domination of the capacities of others, a metaphysics of ruling and being ruled.

While in the distribution warehouse we saw the way in which the repertoire is taken as a means of dominating the life that performs it, in other contexts there are repertoires that are given shape so that lives can better dominate and direct violence toward other lives. Nearby the Tze'elim military base in the Negev desert there is a training center built by the Israeli military that was designed to prepare soldiers for combat in Gaza. Constructed as a mock Arab town with a mosque, central square, alleys, shops, and homes, the architectural space allows for military units to rehearse a range of operations and scenarios in a simulated environment. Soldiers sprint through the streets, jump over barriers, and practice various techniques and formations, executing gestures systematically in repetition so that over time a repertoire is formed. Israeli companies such as Bagira Systems also produce virtual reality equipment and digital training environments that can be deployed in facilities such as the Negev training center, creating simulated enemies to exterminate so that the repertoire can be further given shape and sharpened through computational means. Images of life are produced so actual lives can be killed. These architectural and algorithmic technologies ultimately aim to build up repertoires in soldiers so that when they are eventually deployed in Gaza or the West Bank, they will already have at their disposal sets of instincts, techniques, actions, and reflexes designed to inflict maximum violence. Bodies take on new muscular shapes, and senses and reflexes are honed. The repertoire in this context appears not as an economic but rather as a military technology, as something that must be continuously maintained and manufactured so that when the time comes it can be rapidly deployed to destroy.

While Israel is at the forefront of developing these training programs, there are a range of such projects in the United States as well, including the Atlanta Public Safety Training Center (known as Cop City), which was constructed to train police, as well as a facility at Fort Benning designed to prepare Immigration and Customs Enforcement (ICE) agents to execute mass disappearances and deportations. The private companies that are contracted to build these training centers, such as Strategic Operations Incorporated, highlight the modular nature of the architecture in their marketing materials, claiming that the police and military will be able to train within a reconfigurable and reprogrammable space that provides the possibility of combinatorially expanding the repertoires that are rehearsed within them. Just as military war games are designed to map our various strategics given a range of initial conditions, these training centers offer a means of developing a range of repertoires that can be put to use in a range of scenarios and situations.

The systematic weaponization of the repertoire is one of the reasons police around the world can be recognized so easily, not simply because of their similar uniforms and equipment but also because they enact the same repertoire of gestures when they go on the offensive, organizing themselves into lines and snatch squads, following scripted tactics and rehearsed formations in a largely homogeneous form. In Israel and the United States and across a global network of nation-states, we thus see the simulated violence of the past build up into repertoires that are then actualized to dispense immense amounts of violence in the present and into the future. If in the Amazon warehouse the repertoire is weaponized as a means of subjugating the very same lives that are compelled to perform them, in these simulated training centers the repertoire is weaponized so that some lives are prepared to brutalize and eliminate other lives.

Counterposed to these forms of domination that take the repertoire as their material are practices that take the gesture as something radically opposed to order and constraint, as that which has the potential to liberate and spread disorder rather than dominate and impose order. Across the revolts of the twenty-first century, a wide diversity of repertoires has taken shape, which has then gone on to circulate between revolts, passing back and forth across constellations of struggles. Paradigmatic in this regard were the uprisings in Hong Kong in 2018, which culminated in an astonishingly creative process of invention and experimentation. New shape was given to repertoires that were concerned with creating multilayered lines of defense at the front of marches, rapidly assembling and dispersing in response to police deployments, dearresting people when they were grabbed by the police, and using lasers and throwing projectiles to defend space. Emerging physically on the streets in the tumult of conflict and also emerging sensually as a multiplication of images shared between friends across neighborhoods and cities and then jumping across borders, the gestures and techniques of this uprising would later reappear and take on new shape in uprisings in the United States, Lebanon, Thailand, France, Iran, and other sites of social explosion in the months and years that followed. While in the economy the appearance of the gesture as an image emerges as a means of control, in the context of uprisings a gesture's appearance as an image takes on a different potential as it contagiously spreads to disparate places where people perceive what is unfolding elsewhere and then begin to experiment with it wherever they are. These images rapidly multiply and spread across the network form of society, just as they rapidly jump offline and crash into the streets as they struggle to find new shape and form in relation to the specificities of their context.

Spending time with one of these gestures in particular may help reveal the way in which a gesture finds a place and is developed within a repertoire. Tear gas has proven to be the weapon of choice for many police departments around the world who aspire to quell uprisings by suffocating them in clouds of toxic gas, and as a result finding ways of responding to the use of tear gas has proven to be one of the essential repertoires to be cultivated and popularized within uprisings. The first time you are exposed to tear gas, the instinct is to run, to hold one's breath and flee in whatever direction leads most quickly away from the gas. This frantic and desperate attempt to escape most often results in a dispersion of whatever had been taking place as well as a dramatic increase in vulnerability as crowds fragment into panicked and isolated individuals who are easily brutalized and arrested. One of the first repertoires that begins to take shape in such situations thus simply involves preparing yourself so that you don't run but rather walk and remain calm, creating time to take in your surroundings and then proceed in a different way. Such an elementary shift in gesture is enough to radically transform the situation, holding together those who have gathered, making it possible to defend and take care of one another, and thus creating further time and space for the emergence of other gestures. This switch from running and fleeing to walking and remaining calm thus functions as an action but also an image that can be perceived by those nearby, becoming relational as those who might otherwise run see people around them remain calm and thus find a way of remaining calm themselves.

Once people have developed the repertoire of not panicking or fleeing from the gas and thus of creating time to respond within it, other repertoires then become possible and begin to take form. When tear gas canisters are fired and fall into a crowd, people have learned to throw them back toward the lines of police, a gesture that seems on the surface quite straightforward but in practice involves considerable technique and thus must be practiced and refined like any other art. As tear gas canisters get dangerously hot when they are activated, they not only must be handled with heat-resistant gloves but also must be picked up quickly and released just as fast to avoid being burned or letting the gas spread too far or too thickly. As someone who has developed this repertoire goes to grasp the canister, their whole body leans over and flexes like a bow. Their arm then quickly arcs from the floor over their head in a continuous motion, minimizing the duration the canister is held while releasing it into the air with maximum force as all of the tension that has been built up in the body is released, sending the canister flying along an elegant curve that is an extension of the curve of the body that threw it. The crowd is thus given relief from the gas, and the police must then contend with the effects of the very weapon they had deployed. This gesture of throwing back a tear gas canister takes on further shape each time it's enacted, and thus it steadily builds up into a repertoire, not so different from the way a pirouette in ballet or a riposte in fencing is refined over time.

In Hong Kong an additional repertoire was developed to counter the use of tear gas, involving multiple people collaboratively executing gestures together in a tightly choreographed sequence. As soon as the canister hits the ground, one person covers the canister with a traffic cone while several others douse the area and pour water directly into the open top of the cone, interrupting the flow of the gas quickly and effectively. This particular repertoire has the advantage of freeing others in the crowd to pursue other gestures. Seeing that one group is capable of rapidly and artfully neutralizing the threat of tear gas allows other individuals and groups to engage in all of the other gestures of the revolt, such as dragging things into the street to block police vehicles, attending to injured people in the crowd, or spraying graffiti across the surrounding walls. To rephrase Gilles Deleuze and Baruch Spinoza, the revolt does not concern itself with what *a life is* so much as what *a life can do*, a shift that abandons any need to define or fix the gesture as a thing, as it arises instead as creativity and autonomy and thus as an immense danger to all forms of domination and control.

The physicality and sensuality of the gesture come to take on a completely distinct formal logic as it exits the economy and erupts as revolt. Actions and their appearance no longer are means of capturing and orchestrating life but instead offer a collective intensification of what life can do and be. The things that are done and are seen in an uprising provide the fuel for further experimentation and improvisation, for *an uncontrolled explosion of gestures in revolt* that is oriented principally toward the multiplication of life's potentials. Uprisings are in this sense nothing less than an insurrectionary laboratory of the gesture, allowing forms to become sharpened and elaborated as a consequence of repertoires building on repertoires, and of repertoires clashing against repertoires. The shape of life finds its contours among many lives, just as everyone's freedom is the necessary condition of any one life living freely.

What is clear in retrospect in the case of the uprisings in Hong Kong is that even this creative explosion of new gestures and the militant refinement of repertoires was not enough to defeat the militarized police forces of the Chinese state that had invaded the city. The revolt was in the end brutally repressed, and then the pandemic largely erased its memory from the world's imagination. However, the uprisings of Hong Kong (like all uprisings before and after) still have an immense amount to teach us. One lesson we can learn involves the need to create and defend an open space for the experimentation with and evolution of repertoires, to not allow uprisings to split over some ideal form of action but rather to see the ways in which diverse gestures can build on one another not in a strict and imposed harmony but in a creative and cascading cacophony. Deciding exactly what kinds of repertoires will be allowed within an uprising in advance and then policing uprisings so that they follow the script is a recipe for remaining irrelevant and learning absolutely nothing. The presence of various authoritarian groups within uprisings—whether appearing in the form of liberal peace police who demand everyone endlessly march in circles or party activists intent to control uprisings so they can be the ones to ultimately lead and represent them—is thus nothing more than another constraint that ultimately must be broken by the unruly gestures that are always already circulating and taking shape in these situations.

Another lesson involves the need to spread and multiply the uprising beyond any isolated context, allowing gestures to multiply and mutate into a form that may prove capable of finally overwhelming domination on a global scale. While the form of an uprising in a suburb, town, or metropolis will greatly vary, as will the gestures deployed within them—what arises as a valuable repertoire in Cairo will be quite different than what is needed from a repertoire in Los Angeles, the Susa Valley, or Jenin—it is clear that gestures and repertoires must nonetheless find ways of circulating between these diverse contexts so that they can be adapted and translated into new forms as needed. This planetary transmission of and experimentation with repertoires has become necessary principally because the police and military forces that they oppose also circulate repertoires between them across countries and continents. It is in this sense that the supposed division between "domestic repression" and "foreign operations" is simply a mirage that masks the never-ending elaboration and diffusion of all forms of state violence, emerging as global forms of domination that must be confronted by global forms of revolt. Just as Israeli military forces train riot police in the United States, so too must uprisings find ways of circulating repertoires, gestures, techniques, forms, capacities, and knowledge between them.

Those who took part in the uprisings in Hong Kong compiled what they had learned on the streets into electronic pamphlets that could be read by people everywhere, thus spreading and multiplying repertoires that involved how to remain fluid in the streets, how to dismantle surveillance equipment, how to hold space, how to remedy the effects of chemical weapons, and many others. This practice of developing but also sharing what unfolds in an uprising must be consciously generalized in the years to come, with each repertoire being understood both as action and as image, as practice and as theory, as a repertoire that unfolds on the streets but also as a repertoire that spreads as a concept. It is only through a collective multiplication and refining of repertoires that uprisings can emerge not as a form of disorder that remains fleeting and isolated but as a form of disorder whose scale and force is world historical.

Capitalism's fragmentation and subordination of gestures is a profound assault on life itself, an uncompromising war waged against life and all the creative forces that are involved in living. A fundamental dimension of our autonomy thus can be found in the ways we approach our life *as its own singular gesture*, as a potential continuously unfolding over our lifetimes that is entwined with the potentiality of many other lives. The total atomization of network society that breaks apart this gesture of our lives into ever smaller units subjected to oversight and control results in nothing less than a total disintegration and degradation of what it means to live. Life crumbles into scattered capacities to be measured, calculated, and spent, capacities that are then ordered and organized in ways that are essentially hostile to life and that make it less and less possible to contemplate or value life itself. What is a repertoire? A repertoire is that which capitalism and network society have historically managed to capture and domesticate, to subsume and economize, to train and tame. What is a repertoire? A repertoire is that which must be taken back as a means of living the autonomy and anarchy that is inherent in life, of defending and intensifying all of what in life remains creative, wild, and free.

Acknowledgments

Susana Galán, Jasmine Ehrhardt, Alexander R. Galloway, and Jara Rocha all read drafts of this text, generously provided insightful criticisms and commentaries, and challenged me to pursue paths that I would have been unable to follow without their sharp commitments and profound intellects, for which I will always be greatly appreciative. La Virreina Centre de la Imatge in Barcelona also invited me to present excerpts of this project while it was still in an early form, which proved immensely useful as I was completing its final sections. I would also like to express my sincere gratitude to PM Press, who salvaged *The Reticular Society* after it was left adrift. In particular, Joey Paxman was instrumental to seeing the project all the way through the publication process, ensuring that every step was taken thoughtfully and with great care. Wade Ostrowski also was of crucial assistance during the editing stages, attentively and artfully helping to polish, clarify, and refine the entire manuscript. And finally, this project wouldn't exist without all of those who sustain the unrivaled beauty of a life that refuses to dominate or be dominated, all of those who remind us of what it means to live.

About the Contributors

Ian Alan Paul is a theorist whose work engages with technopolitics and anarchist thought. They live in Barcelona, where they teach in the Graduate Program in Media, Power, and Difference at Pompeu Fabra University.

Serene Richards is the author of *Biopolitics as a System of Thought*, published by Bloomsbury Academic in 2024. She teaches law at NYU London and writes on legal and political theory and contemporary philosophy.

ABOUT PM PRESS

PM Press is an independent, radical publisher of critically necessary books for our tumultuous times. Our aim is to deliver bold political ideas and vital stories to all walks of life and arm the dreamers to demand the impossible. Founded in 2007 by a small group of people with decades of publishing, media, and organizing experience, we have sold millions of copies of our books, most often one at a time, face to face. We're old enough to know what we're doing and young enough to know what's at stake. Join us to create a better world.

PM Press
PO Box 23912
Oakland, CA 94623
www.pmpress.org

PM Press in Europe
europe@pmpress.org
www.pmpress.org.uk

FRIENDS OF PM PRESS

These are indisputably momentous times—the financial system is melting down globally and the Empire is stumbling. Now more than ever there is a vital need for radical ideas.

In the many years since its founding—and on a mere shoestring—PM Press has risen to the formidable challenge of publishing and distributing knowledge and entertainment for the struggles ahead. With hundreds of releases to date, we have published an impressive and stimulating array of literature, art, music, politics, and culture. Using every available medium, we've succeeded in connecting those hungry for ideas and information to those putting them into practice.

Friends of PM allows you to directly help impact, amplify, and revitalize the discourse and actions of radical writers, filmmakers, and artists. It provides us with a stable foundation from which we can build upon our early successes and provides a much-needed subsidy for the materials that can't necessarily pay their own way. You can help make that happen—and receive every new title automatically delivered to your door once a month—by joining as a Friend of PM Press. And, we'll throw in a free T-shirt when you sign up.

Here are your options:

- **$30 a month** Get all books and pamphlets plus a 50% discount on all webstore purchases
- **$40 a month** Get all PM Press releases (including CDs and DVDs) plus a 50% discount on all webstore purchases
- **$100 a month** Superstar—Everything plus PM merchandise, free downloads, and a 50% discount on all webstore purchases

For those who can't afford $30 or more a month, we have **Sustainer Rates** at $15, $10 and $5. Sustainers get a free PM Press T-shirt and a 50% discount on all purchases from our website.

Your Visa or Mastercard will be billed once a month, until you tell us to stop. Or until our efforts succeed in bringing the revolution around. Or the financial meltdown of Capital makes plastic redundant. Whichever comes first.

The Society of the Spectacle (PM Edition)

Guy Debord
Edited and translated by Ken Knabb

ISBN: 979-8-88744-056-9
$19.95 160 pages

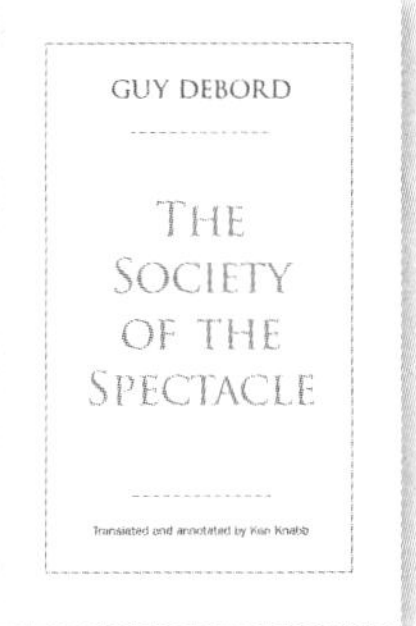

The Society of the Spectacle is a carefully considered effort to clarify the most fundamental tendencies and contradictions of the society in which we find ourselves—in order to facilitate its overthrow.

Guy Debord was the founder of the Situationist International, the notorious avant-garde group that helped trigger the May 1968 revolt in France, which brought the entire country to a standstill for several weeks. His book *The Society of the Spectacle*, originally published in Paris in 1967, has been translated into more than twenty other languages and is arguably the most important radical work of the twentieth century. Ken Knabb's meticulous new translation is the first edition in any language to include extensive annotations, clarifying the historical allusions and revealing the sources of Debord's quotations and "détournements."

Contrary to popular misconceptions, Debord's book is neither an ivory-tower philosophical discourse nor a mere expression of "protest." This makes the book more of a challenge, but it is also why it remains so pertinent more than half a century after its original publication, while countless other social theories and intellectual fads have come and gone.

It has, in fact, become even more pertinent than ever, because the spectacle has become more all-pervading and glaringly obvious than ever. As Debord noted in his follow-up work, *Comments on the Society of the Spectacle* (1988), "Spectacular domination has succeeded in raising an entire generation molded to its laws." Debord's book remains the best guidebook to understanding that mold and breaking it.

"I read The Society of the Spectacle *again and I thought, 'This is a fucking amazing book!' I had forgotten how terrific it was, and it was actually quite different to how I remembered it. I insist that the key chapter is not the first one, on the spectacle itself, but the second to last—the chapter on détournement. To me, that concept is the great gift of the Situationists. They realized that one can exploit this critically—one can copy and correct in the direction of hope."*
—McKenzie Wark, author of *A Hacker Manifesto*, in *Los Angeles Review of Books*

Situationist International Anthology (PM Edition)

Edited and translated by Ken Knabb

ISBN: 979-8-88744-057-6
$29.95 544 pages

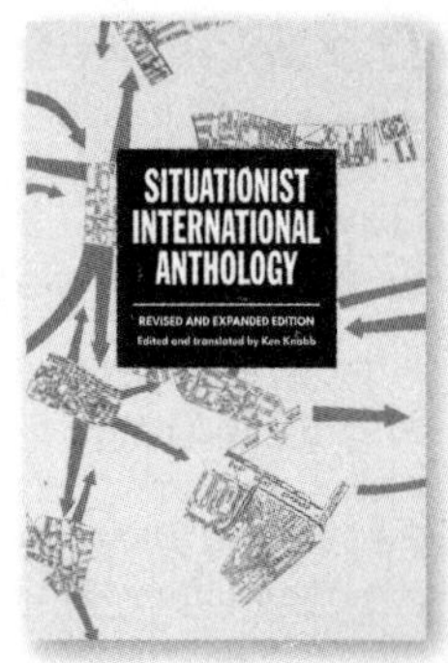

In 1957 a few European avant-garde groups came together to form the Situationist International. Picking up where the dadaists and surrealists had left off, the situationists challenged people's passive conditioning with carefully calculated scandals and the playful tactic of *détournement*. Seeking a more extreme social revolution than was dreamed of by most leftists, they developed an incisive critique of the global spectacle-commodity system and of its "Communist" pseudo-opposition, and their new methods of agitation helped trigger the May 1968 revolt in France. Since then situationist theories and tactics have continued to inspire radical currents all over the world.

The *Situationist International Anthology* is the most comprehensive and accurately translated collection of situationist writings in English. It presents a rich variety of articles, leaflets, graffiti, and internal documents, ranging from experiments in "psychogeography" to lucid analyses of the Watts riots, the Vietnam War, the Prague Spring, the Chinese Cultural Revolution, and other crises and upheavals of the sixties.

For this new edition all the translations have been fine-tuned and the bibliography has been updated to include comments on dozens of newer books by and about the situationists.